No-Fuss
Wood Finishing

No-Fuss
Wood Finishing

TIPS, TECHNIQUES & SECRETS FROM THE PROS
for Expert Results

Edited by Randy Johnson

FOX CHAPEL
PUBLISHING

Published by Fox Chapel Publishing Company, Inc., 1970 Broad St., East Petersburg, PA 17520, 717-560-4703, www.FoxChapelPublishing.com

American Woodworker, ISSN 1074-9152, USPS 738-710, is published bimonthly by Woodworking Media, LLC, 90 Sherman St., Cambridge, MA 02140, *www.AmericanWoodworker.com*.

Library of Congress Control Number:
ISBN-13: 978-1-56523-747-6
ISBN-10: 1-56523-747-1

Library of Congress Cataloging-in-Publication Data

No-fuss wood finishing. -- First [edition].

        pages cm

 Includes index.

Summary: "Amateur woodworkers can achieve professional-quality finishes on their projects with simple materials that are brushed or wiped onto the wood. There's no need to shell out for expensive professional spray equipment nor to invest the hours required to use it. The secrets in this book include focusing on brushable polyurethane varnish, brushable shellac, and wipe-on glaze coats. Readers will learn how to use and clean a fine finishing brush, when to brush and when to wipe the finish on, and how to get a flawless finish without the tedious labor of rubbing out. Includes detailed instructions for matching colors with simple stains, how to make nondescript woods such as poplar look great, and how to apply a glaze coat for professional highlights on carvings, moldings and other details. Includes a special section on reviving damaged finishes, erasing water-damage, and when all else fails, how to strip off the old finish and start over. "-- Provided by publisher.

ISBN 978-1-56523-747-6 (pbk.)

1. Wood finishing. I. American woodworker.

TT325.N64 2012

745.51--dc23

2012018158

To learn more about the other great books from Fox Chapel Publishing, or to find a retailer near you, call toll-free 800-457-9112 or visit us at *www.FoxChapelPublishing.com*.

Printed in China
First printing

On the cover: A thick gel stain acts as a glaze to give this molding depth and definition. More on page 72.

Frontispiece: When you're building furniture, it's simplest to pre-finish the parts before assembly. Page 41.

Contents

What You Can Learn

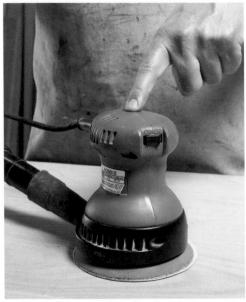

Sanding prepares the surface. Surface preparation is the key to a fine finish, and sanding is the key to surface preparation. It doesn't have to be fierce work. See pages 23 through 27.

Varnish for durability. Varnish is the most versatile and durable finish that you can apply without a lot of fuss. Varnish finish can take any sheen from satin to high gloss, it can be brushed on or wiped on with a rag. Lots more detailed information to help you choose the most appropriate type of varnish for your project, and how to get the best results, pages 41 through 71.

Shellac for beauty. Shellac is the traditional finish for fine furniture, and there are many ways to use shellac in the finishing process. See pages 28 through 40 and pages 111 though 114, as well as tips scattered throughout the book.

Coloring the wood. You can learn how to match colors and finishes using step boards (pages 80 through 91), how to put a fine finish on ordinary poplar, and how to finish such difficult woods as cherry and golden oak (pages 91 through 105). Then add richness and depth to any finish using gel stains as glazes (page 106).

Cleaning the brush. You paid a lot for that fine finishing brush, it really works great, but now it's time to clean it and store it away safely, ready for next time you need it, page 18.

Repairing damaged finishes. Before you can repair a damaged finish, you need to determine whether the trouble is in the finish, or beneath it in the wood itself (page 119). You'll find scores of useful techniques for repairing the damage with minimal intervention (page 120 through 133), but when all else fails, you might have to strip off the old finish and start anew (page 134).

Finishing Techniques

F inishing wood may seem hopelessly complicated, mysterious, and expensive, but it's not. You can get perfect results in your home workshop, using brushes, wiping rags, and readily available materials. For durability and versatility, it's hard to beat polyurethane varnish, in either an oil- or water-based formulation. And for the finest furniture, there's no finish more beautiful than a French polish, that is, many coats of shellac rubbed out to the precise sheen you want.

Like most woodworking processes, successful finishing get easier when you put attention on learning good techniques and working habits. This section gives you the foundation of techniques and information that you need.

You've got to finish all of it—every surface. These simple levitators lift the piece so you can get at it and see what you are doing, page 17.

by KEVIN SOUTHWICK

Pro's Guide to 30 Finishing Supplies

30 MUST-HAVE TOOLS FOR FINISHING ALL TYPES OF WOODWORKING PROJECTS

Collecting woodworking tools is undeniably fun. As a professional finisher, I meet a lot of woodworkers on the job and in the classes that I teach. So I know that spending hundreds of dollars on a new router or a fine hand plane is thought of as a reasonable expense for an essential tool. On the other hand, having to buy sandpaper or a new can of finish is usually likened to throwing money away.

Why is that? I think of finishing supplies as good investments—essential woodworking tools on a par with those that cut and shape wood. Good finishing tools make it easier to apply good finishes, which both improves my enjoyment of woodworking and produces a superior result. In my opinion, a well-equipped woodworking shop includes a well-equipped finishing cabinet. Here's a collection of finishing tools and supplies that I think are worthy of your hard-earned cash.

Touch-Up Tools

Knowing how to hide mistakes makes you a better woodworker. Touch-up tools allow you to disguise defects such as glue spots, sanded through edges, light-colored scratches, and fill-ins that don't quite match. **Wood touch-up pens** are handy to have, as are **colored pencils** and wood-tone **colored markers** from an art materials or office supply store.

Here are all of the tools, supplies, and materials you'll need for finishing success. This story takes your finishing kit apart and discusses your choices in each category.

EDITOR: TIM JOHNSON

Finishes You Can Wipe, Brush or Spray

It makes sense to keep different kinds of finish on hand, because each project presents unique finishing challenges. **A wipe-on/wipe-off finish**, such as General Finishes Gel Topcoat urethane, looks great, applies easily and eliminates worries about bubbles, drips, runs, sags, dust nibs, hair, or brush marks. Any finishing oil, oil/varnish blend, or gel varnish will do, as long as you prepare the surface well and buff the finish thoroughly dry, to avoid streaks. Wipe-on/wipe-off finishes leave an attractive low sheen, but they provide limited water resistance and numerous applications may be required.

Film-building finish, such as Varathane oil-based polyurethane, is the best choice if you want a higher sheen or better moisture protection. Building a film finish requires a brush or pad, sanding between coats, and a little practice. Most oil-based polyurethanes can be thinned to make wipe-on/wipe-off finishes.

Shellac is a must-have. A beautiful finish on its own, shellac can also be a big time-saver, because it dries super-fast. Zinnser SealCoat is liquid shellac that's light in color and free of wax, so it's compatible with virtually any other finish.

Spray-on finish in aerosol cans is excellent for finishing smaller projects. Many different finishes are available as aerosols, including lacquer, shellac, acrylic and polyurethane. Apply thin coats for the best results.

Washable Dust Mask

Organic Vapor Cartridge

Dust Mask and Respirator

A reusable dust mask is worth the initial investment, because it can last for years. Just wash it by hand and it's ready to reuse. Dust Bee Gone brand reusable masks are comfortable and much more effective than any paper disposable masks I have ever used.

A respirator mask with organic vapor cartridges is a must-have to limit your exposure to toxic fumes found in finishing products. Lay in a supply of cartridges and replace them regularly.

Varnish

Sash

Disposable

Synthetic

4 Types of Brushes

When you choose a finishing brush, consider the task you want to perform. For example, when you are applying varnish, you'll get the best results by using a varnish brush, rather than a paint brush. **A varnish brush** is designed and constructed to be used with thin finishes such as oil-based polyurethane, shellac and lacquer; paint brushes are designed to apply much thicker material. The best varnish brushes have very fine natural bristles that are relatively short and densely packed. A 2"-wide brush is the most versatile size.

Redtree and Gramercy natural bristle varnish brushes are my favorites. Redtree 2" brushes cost about the same as a paint brush of comparable size and quality. Gramercy brushes cost twice as much, but they're made by hand and are worth every penny.

A sash brush is a round, tapered natural bristle brush that is uniquely suited for evenly applying finishes to uneven surfaces such as shaped moldings or carvings. I keep a range of sizes ready for use. Sash brushes are available at art materials stores.

A synthetic bristle brush, made with Taklon nylon bristles, is an excellent choice for water based materials.

Disposable brushes are indispensable: No cleaning required! Chip brushes (natural bristle) are useful for applying both stains and finishes (although they do shed bristles). Foam brushes work well on flat surfaces. However, shellac and lacquer will dissolve them.

Information for Your Brain

Creating a great finish begins before you even open a can. **Books about finishing wood** are loaded with useful information, techniques and formulas, facts and honest opinions. I've learned something new from every finishing book that I've read. Bob Flexner's *Understanding Wood Finishing* is comprehensive and well organized. It also has an excellent in-depth index that's helpful whether you're seeking general information or trying to solve a specific problem.

Surface Preparation Tools

Any tool that makes sanding faster or easier is welcome in my shop. Machine sanders are obviously important, but even the best leave marks that must be removed for a top-quality finish. That's why hand sanding blocks are the most frequently used tools in my shop.

Shop-made sanding blocks of ¾" wood with ¼" cork or neoprene glued on the business end are my favorites for use on bare wood. Cork's firmness works best for flattening; neoprene works best for subtle curves or easing an edge. I keep several different sizes and shapes to meet needs such as reaching into tight corners.

The Preppin' Weapon is a good choice for sanding large flat surfaces; **solid cork blocks** work well for general sanding.

Hard felt or dense neoprene blocks work best for sanding film finishes between coats. These materials have flexible, cushioned working surfaces that provide consistent and delicate control.

Task Lighting

A movable light source, such as this inexpensive clamp light, is especially helpful to have during sanding and finishing operations. Highlighting surfaces with light from raking angles reveals defects and problems much more clearly than overhead light. Good overhead lighting is also important. Be aware that colors look different under different types of lighting. Incandescent light makes colors appear "warmer" than natural light and fluorescent light makes colors appear "cooler." For this reason, color matching should always be done under the same type of lighting in which the final results will be viewed.

Wood Coloring Materials

Changing the natural color of wood is optional; if you want to do it, you should be familiar with two types of stains.

Pigmented oil stains in liquid or gel form are usually the easiest wood colorants to use. Gel stains are especially good for color matching, because they can be used like a glaze for layering color. Stains and glazes made using artist's oil colors offer the widest choice of colors. To make your own liquid stain, mix the oil colors in a 2 to 1 solution of mineral spirits and boiled linseed oil. To make a glaze, mix the oil colors with glazing medium. Artist's oil colors and glazing medium are available at art materials stores.

Dye stains are unique because they have both powerful and subtle coloring abilities. For example, they can turn maple jet black, gently tint it to an aged golden tone or amplify its curly figure. Water-soluble dyes are the easiest to use on bare wood and are usually the best choice for accentuating highly figured woods.

Liquid
Gel
Glazing Medium
Water Dyes
Artist's Oils

Dust Collection

An effective shop vacuum traps dust without re-circulating small particles, which can ruin your finishes, back into the air. Fein vacuums come with cloth filters that remove dust particles down to 5 microns, and finer filters are available as upgrades.

A room air filtration system, usually installed to remove fine airborne dust for health reasons, will also clean the air before you apply finishes. Run the system for an hour or two and shut it off just before finishing begins.

Rags and Cloths

Scott brand shop rags are my top choice for general use. These lint-free, heavy-duty paper towels are economical and available in rolls or boxes—I prefer the boxes, because they keep the towels clean.

Knit 100% cotton rags are more absorbent than towels. They're good for staining and for wipe-on/wipe-off finishes. Buy them ready for use or cut them from 100% cotton T-shirts—just avoid the seams, collars and armbands.

Super absorbent, **100% cotton cheesecloth** makes an excellent applicator pad that affords precise control for padding or wiping on film-building finishes. Wrap a pad of cheesecloth in nylon stocking fabric for an extra-nice applicator.

Micro-fiber tack cloths make traditional tack cloths obsolete. They grab and hold dust amazingly well, and they're infinitely reusable. I use two—one that's dry, for initial dusting, and one that's barely damp, for use immediately before applying finish.

Top Quality Abrasives

High-tech sandpaper is made with durable backing paper, no-load coatings, and abrasive particles that stay sharp and are consistently sized. This sandpaper cuts quickly, leaves a uniform scratch pattern and lasts a long time. Stock ample supplies of sandpaper in every grit that you commonly use. Buy only the best quality paper, such as Norton 3X or 3M Sandblaster.

Steel wool ranges in quality, too. For example, the steel wool you find at hardware stores can be quite oily as a result of the manufacturing process. Top brands, such as Liberon, have very consistent, long, fine strands of steel that last longer, and don't shred as easily, so they are less messy.

Nylon abrasive pads (also called synthetic steel wool) are an alternative to using fine sandpaper or 0000 steel wool between coats of finish. Abrasive pads don't leave steel fibers behind, but they also don't cut as consistently as good quality steel wool.

Levitators

Brushing around the bottom of furniture legs is awkward. It's hard to see what you're doing, so it's easy to miss spots or lay on a coat that's too heavy. It's also hard to keep your brush from touching the workbench. If your brush gets contaminated, your finish can be ruined.

Simple-to-make "levitators" make this job much easier. By raising your workpiece off the workbench, they give more room to maneuver the brush. A slight tap on the top of each leg sets the screw points—pick up the workpiece and the levitators remain attached. This makes it easy to reposition the piece while you're working on it or move it out of the way when you're done.

Drywall screws work best because they have very sharp points. (Standard wood screws don't work.) Levitators are handy to have around, so make a bunch. Just stick them in a piece of rigid foam insulation board for storage so you won't get jabbed by the points!

Kevin O'Donnell

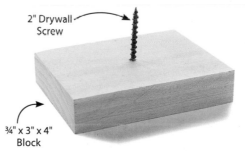

2" Drywall Screw

¾" x 3" x 4" Block

ART DIRECTION: JOEL SPIES · PHOTOGRAPHY: KRIVIT PHOTOGRAPHY · CONSULTANT: MICHAEL DRESDNER

by SCOTT HOLMES

Brush Care 101

HOW TO CHOOSE, CONDITION AND CLEAN A FINISHING BRUSH

It's really tempting to buy an inexpensive brush for finishing. Say you spend a few dollars on a standard paint brush and throw it away rather than taking the time to clean it. You may buy 40 such brushes over the next 10 years…that's more than a few dollars! A much better plan is to buy one or two high-quality finishing brushes and take care of them. This is a win-win proposition: Not only do you save big bucks, your finishes will look like a million bucks, too.

A high-quality brush is a joy to use, because it distributes finish evenly,

Hang cleaned brushes in plastic sleeves, and they are ready to go again.

leaving a consistent layer on the surface, without any brush marks. It won't lose bristles and it holds more finish than a standard brush, so you're not constantly reloading it. Once you've used a high-quality finishing brush, you'll never go back.

It's true that cleaning a brush is a chore. Well, so is washing the dog, but he sure smells better afterwards! My point is that there's a reward: Take care of your brush and it will last a lifetime. In fact, just like a good bottle of wine, a high-quality brush will get better with age. Here's how to choose and care for a brush for applying film-forming finishes such as oil-based polyurethane varnish.

Features of a High-Quality Brush

A thick head. The more bristles a brush has, the more finish it can hold and the better it will flow the finish onto the wood. A high-quality finishing brush has a visibly thick head that probably contains three to four times the number of bristles in a standard brush (Photo 1, next page). Standard brush heads have a hollow reservoir in the middle, because they're designed to apply thick paint. Varnish is thinner, so a high-quality finishing brush has no such hollow space.

Soft, flexible bristles. The stiffer the bristles, the longer they must be to flex enough to lay down the finish. The longer the bristles, the more difficult a brush is to control.

Choose a brush with natural bristles for oil-based varnish. Natural bristles are usually China bristle, ox hair or a combination of the two. China bristle is Chinese boar hair, a long, tapered hair that works well for oil-based varnish. China bristles are naturally black or white—the white bristles are a bit finer and softer. The best China bristles are sometimes dyed to imitate badger hair (a superb bristle that's become so expensive it's rarely used in finishing brushes). One of my favorite brushes has China bristles that are dyed this way.

Ox hair bristles are finer, softer and more flexible than China bristles. They're usually shorter, too, to optimize control. Ox hair bristles are especially good for detail work, because they flow beautifully over and around contoured surfaces.

A hand-sculpted tip. A tip that's chisel-shaped allows more bristles to contact the surface, resulting in a smoother flow of finish. The high-quality brush maker actually binds the hairs in this shape while forming the brush. Cutting the bristles to create the shape after the brush is bound defeats the advantage of using naturally tapered hairs.

Brushes that are 2" wide are the workhorses in my shop, because they're the most versatile. For large, flat surfaces, though, I often use wider brushes.

A heavy-gauge ferrule. High-quality brushes have thick ferrules made of metal that won't rust; the best are stainless steel.

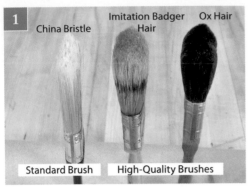

The head of a high-quality brush will be thick and hand-shaped to a chisel point. Look for bristles made from top-quality China bristle (sometimes called "imitation badger hair") or ox hair.

A quick soak before each use fills the bristles and coats them with mineral spirits, so the varnish flows easily from the brush onto the surface. Watch as you insert the brush—you can actually see the solvent wick up the bristles.

A four-step rinse with previously used mineral spirits removes the varnish. Notice that the solvent in the three rinse containers gets clearer as the brush gets cleaner. Use fresh mineral spirits for the last rinse only.

A Quick Soak Conditions The Bristles

One simple step ensures the varnish will flow smoothly from your brush onto the surface. Before each use, soak the bristles in mineral spirits to fill them and coat them all the way up into the ferrule (Photo 2). After a minute or two, gently flex the brush against the side of the container to remove the excess solvent. There's no need to shake or spin the brush, because the goal is to leave solvent in the bristles. Now your brush is ready to apply varnish. And cleaning is easier when the job is done, because the varnish won't get up into the ferrule.

Tip: It's best to use a brush for only one type of finish, so don't use your varnish brush for anything but varnish.

How To Clean and Maintain Your Brush

Cleaning isn't glamorous, but it takes less than 10 minutes to do the job right, and it's rewarding how soft and luxurious the bristles feel at the end of the process. It may help to whistle while you work.

Stage 1: Remove the Varnish

Start with a four-step rinse to remove the varnish (Photo 3). This system reuses mineral spirits from previous cleanings for all but the last rinse—and it cleans your varnishing pan at the same time. Tip: To keep from contaminating an entire can of varnish, always work from a pan rather than the can. And when the job is done, never pour the varnish remaining in the pan back into the can.

After emptying the pan, wipe it with a paper towel to remove any remaining varnish. Then gently pour a few ounces of the first-rinse mineral spirits into the pan. This previously-used solvent can be used again because it's been stored long enough to let the varnish from the previous cleaning settle to the bottom of the container.

Vigorously work the brush in the mineral spirits. The goal is to remove as much varnish as possible. Sweep the bottom and the edges of the pan as you work. Shake out the brush and pour the dirty mineral spirits back into the first-rinse container. Then repeat the process using the second-rinse mineral spirits and again using the third rinse.

After three rinses the brush is nearly clean. Wipe out the pan with a clean paper towel and rinse the brush one more time, using fresh mineral spirits. When you're finished, pour these spirits into the third-rinse container. If you see any color in the solvent after this fourth rinse, do it again. Store the three containers until the varnish has settled out, and they'll be ready for the next cleaning.

Stage 2: Remove the Mineral Spirits

Mineral spirits can leave an oily residue, so to thoroughly clean the bristles you have to remove all the mineral spirits. To do this, I recommend giving the spirits a double-whammy. Start by spraying citrus cleaner into the bristles, working it through the brush and rinsing it out with water (Photo 4). Next, squirt dishwashing soap into the bristles and vigorously work them into the

Citrus cleaner removes most of the mineral spirits. Spray it into the bristles and work it through. Then rinse it out.

Dishwashing soap removes any mineral spirits the citrus cleaner missed. Work the bristles hard to work up a lather and dislodge any loose bristles. Then thoroughly rinse the brush.

Spin the brush to fan the bristles and shed the excess water.

Wrap the brush in a shop towel to hold its shape. Then hang it up to dry.

palm of your hand (Photo 5). It's OK to really give the bristles a workout. Grab them and pull them, so the cleaning process also removes any loose bristles. Thoroughly rinse the brush and then repeat the process. The soap will lather much more easily the second time, an indication that the bristles are clean. Make sure to rinse all the soap from the brush before you proceed to the next

step. Keep working the bristles even after you think the brush is soap-free—you'll be amazed how long suds keep forming.

Shake out the brush and then spin it to remove the water it still holds (Photo 6). Spinning fans the brush head. Work your fingers through the damp bristles to reshape the head, or use a brush comb. Notice that the bristles feel soft and clean, like your hair feels after shampooing. Wrap the brush in a paper towel (Photo 7). Then hang it up and let it dry for at least 24 hours. As water makes natural bristles go limp, the brush won't be usable again until the bristles are completely dry.

Keep the brush wrapped in the paper towel until the next use or transfer it to a cardboard or plastic sleeve for traveling to a jobsite. When you remove the brush, it will be soft and flexible, as good or better than new.

Short Term Storage

There's no need to completely clean the brush if you plan to use it again within a day or two. Instead, just complete Stage 1 of the cleaning process described above to remove all the varnish. Then suspend the brush in fresh mineral spirits. Make sure the bristles don't touch the bottom. This is different from conditioning the bristles for a few minutes before using the brush (Photo 2). Letting the brush stand on the bottom of a container for an extended length of time will distort the bristles.

Bristles Suspended Above the Bottom

SANDING—FINISHING'S ESSENTIAL FIRST STEP

"Nothing affects the final finish as much as sanding does," according to furnituremaker Mark Love. "For years, I applied oil finishes on my pieces. Oil finishes benefit from sanding to very fine grits, so I learned some important sanding lessons. I learned to work through the grits without skipping and to change paper frequently, to make sure that it's always abrading the surface. Sanding with worn-out paper is never a good idea. I use a block to sand flat surfaces; Dura-Block hard foam sanding blocks are my favorites.

"I sand slightly diagonally, and change directions whenever I change grits. This makes it easy to see when all the scratches from the previous grit have been removed. When I sand with the final grit, I follow the grain, and finish by slightly rounding over the sharp outside edges by hand, without using a block.

"To ensure perfect sanding in even the tightest places, I finish-sand each part before I glue anything together— except for glue surfaces and boards for a table top or panel, which I sand after they're glued together.

"I now use clear lacquer as a finish. Like other film-forming finishes such as varnish and polyurethane, lacquer is much more durable than oil finish. To prepare dense hardwoods such as bubinga (shown here) for a film-forming finish, I start with 80 grit sandpaper and work through 100, 120, 180, and 220 grit, before finishing with 320 grit."

Mark sees a difference in the final appearance when he sands dense hardwoods to 320 grit, but some finish manufacturers don't recommend sanding beyond 220 grit, especially if you plan to stain the wood, or if you're working with soft woods such as butternut or pine. So check the label of the finish you plan to use and follow the surface preparation instructions.

As I sand a part, I stop and hold it up to the light. In the reflection I can see whether or not I've removed the scratches from the previous grit.

The part on the left has been sanded all the way to 320 grit. The part on the right has only been sanded to 180 grit. Clearly, 180 grit scratches are so coarse they make the wood look dull.

After sanding, the wood shines…even without finish.

by TIM JOHNSON

Sanding for a Stained Finish

10 TIPS TO MAKE STAIN LOOK GREAT

You're in for a surprise if you think that you can go easy on sanding because you're planning to use stain. Sanding for a stained finish is actually more demanding than sanding for a clear finish, because most stains color wood by lodging in crevices in the surface—and sanding scratches are pretty large crevices. The trick is to eliminate scratches that staining will highlight, such as big scratches from coarse grit, swirls from power sanding or scratches that run across the grain. Here are 10 sanding tips that will make a stained finish look its best.

Go E-Z on the R-O

Random-orbit sanders employ a dual-action motion (the disc rotates and oscillates) to create a uniform scratch pattern that minimizes visible scratches. Bearing down and moving fast while using this type of sander feels natural, but it's the wrong thing to do because it disrupts the sander's dual-action motion and creates uneven scratch patterns. Noticeable scratch marks are the unfortunate result. To keep scratch marks at bay, random-orbit sander manufacturers recommend moving the sander very slowly, about 5 to 10 seconds to cover 6", and applying only light pressure, about 2 to 4 lbs., which is about the weight of your arm.

PHOTOGRAPHY: JASON ZENTNER

Always Sand by Hand

Hand sanding with the grain should always be your last step before applying stain. Power sanding may be a real time-saver, but it rarely leaves surfaces that are entirely scratch-free. Hand sanding after power sanding aligns all the sanding scratches so that the grain will help to hide them. Bearing down when you sand by hand is OK. In fact, it speeds up the process. Using a cork-faced sanding block helps to evenly distribute the sanding pressure. Start with the same grit size that you used for your last round of power sanding. If visible scratches from power sanding remain after hand sanding, switch to slightly coarser grit and start again.

Cork Face

Know When to Sand Further

One way to keep end grain from going dark when stain is applied is to sand it to finer grit than the face grain. On most woods, the end grain is considerably harder than the face grain, which makes sanding scratches and other crevices harder to remove. As a result, the end grain looks darker when it's stained. On the samples shown here (top), the end grain and face grain on the bottom board have both been sanded to 180 grit, while the top board's end grain has been sanded to 320 grit to completely remove the sanding scratches. When stain is applied (bottom), it's clear that the extra sanding pays off: The end grain's color is much more similar to the face grain. The end grain looks better, too—whether it's stained or under a clear finish—because the annual ring structure shows clearly and distinctly.

Sanded to 320 Grit

Sanded to 180 Grit

Moldings Require Sanding

Resist the temptation to stain moldings without sanding them. Even if they feel smooth, moldings often contain milling marks on the raw wood. These marks can be very hard to see because of the wood's grain and the molding's curved surfaces. But if you don't eliminate them by sanding, they'll show up as bands of parallel lines when you stain.

Mill Marks

Sand the Stiles Last

Beware of sanding across joints on stile-and-rail and face-frame assemblies. The goal of sanding by hand is to hide scratches by aligning them with the grain. But going too far on these joints makes the scratches stand out like a sore thumb. To avoid this problem, simply sand the stiles last—and when you sand the stiles, be careful not to cross the joint line, or you'll leave unsightly cross-grain scratches on the end of the rail. On miter joints, sand to the joint line from each direction.

Raise the Grain

Water-based dyes and stains often leave a rough surface because they cause wood fibers bent over by sanding to swell and stand up. The best way to avoid this problem is to preemptively raise and flatten the grain. Then it won't happen when stain is applied. Dampen the wood and let it dry. Then smooth the surface by sanding very lightly with the same grit used for final sanding.

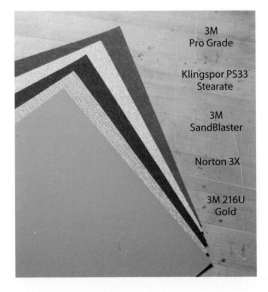

3M Pro Grade

Klingspor PS33 Stearate

3M SandBlaster

Norton 3X

3M 216U Gold

Buy Colored Sandpaper

The best material for sanding unfinished wood is made with premium aluminum oxide abrasive that's graded for consistent size, applied in an open coat, resin-bonded to a flexible lightweight backing and covered with an anti-clogging material. So how do you choose the right stuff? Many manufacturers use color to brand their top-quality sheets, so one easy way is to look for paper that's a distinctive color. Norton 3X, Klingspor PS33 Stearate, 3M 216U Gold, 3M SandBlaster, and 3M Pro Grade all fit the bill. Ironically, sandpaper in shades of brown—the color of sand—is often made with garnet abrasive, which dulls much more quickly than aluminum oxide, so it isn't the best choice. This paper isn't likely to be covered with an anti-clogging material, either.

Know When to Quit

Sanding to super-fine grits makes wood look great under a clear oil finish, but it can cause problems if you plan to use stain. Most oil-based stains contain pigments, which color wood by lodging in pores and other crevices in the surface—such as sanding scratches. As these crevices decrease in size, the stain becomes less effective. Many stain manufacturers recommend finish sanding to 220 grit at most and stopping at a lower grit for a darker color. The samples at right show the difference in stain penetration on mahogany between stopping at 180 grit (left) and sanding to 320 grit (right).

Sanded to 180 Grit   Sanded to 320 Grit

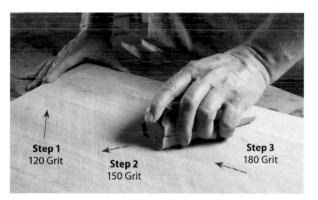

Step 1
120 Grit

Step 2
150 Grit

Step 3
180 Grit

Sand Diagonally

An old-school method for eliminating visible scratch marks is to purposefully make them visible by sanding across the grain as you work your way through the grits. After sanding diagonally in one direction, change to finer grit and sand diagonally in the opposite direction until the scratches from the previous grit disappear. Step up another grit and sand with the grain until all the diagonal scratches are gone.

Pre-sand and Pre-stain

Want to create a finishing time bomb? Just wait to sand and stain frame-and-panel structures after they're assembled. During the heating season, the panel is likely to shrink because of the lower humidity, exposing a strip of unfinished wood at one or both edges. To hide the panel's seasonal movement, sand, stain and finish it before assembling the frame-and-panel structure.

by MITCH KOHANEK

Brushing Shellac

APPLY SHELLAC LIKE A PRO

On flat surfaces, brush on multiple coats of thinned shellac.

If you aren't brushing shellac these days, it's either because you've never tried it or you've had a bad experience. Let's see if I can change that.

The number one reason people abandon shellac is they expect it to behave like polyurethane. But shellac and poly are different animals. For starters, shellac uses fast-drying 200-proof grain alcohol, or ethanol, as a solvent. The non-toxic ethanol is "poisoned" with small amounts of toxic solvent such as methanol or acetone in order to render it undrinkable and escape liquor taxes. Ethanol evaporates quickly and requires a different method of application and tools than slow- drying polyurethane varnishes.

A skilled professional can make brushing on any type of coating look easy. But, like any skill, applying shellac takes practice. Were your first hand-cut dovetails perfect?

Practice brushing on a two-foot square panel before you touch anything of value. It's easy to sand the panel back down to the wood and brush it again and again. After you get comfortable with brushing the panel, go to a garage sale and purchase a small table or chair. Lightly sand it with some 320 grit sandpaper and practice brushing on real furniture.

Shellac's Advantages

There are two reasons for using any finish: The first is to enhance or change the original appearance of the wood; the second is to protect it.

Shellac creates a warmth and depth that makes inexpensive woods look expensive and expensive woods look even more impressive. So you're covered on the good looks front. As a rule of thumb, use light colored shellac on light woods and a dark colored shellac on darker woods.

Let's look at the protection issue. Many people refrain from using shellac because they've heard it offers little protection. But how much protection does the project really need, and from what? A kitchen table needs a whole lot more protection than a jewelry box or a grandfather clock. Shellac may not be the best choice for a kitchen table but for many other projects shellac offers plenty of protection. Besides beauty and protection, shellac has other distinct advantages: Unlike polyurethane, shellac is repairable and can be fixed without stripping off the old finish. Also, shellac's rapid cure leaves little time for dust to settle into the wet finish and you can recoat in less than an hour. Finally, shellac does not require sanding between coats saving you time and elbow grease.

In recent years, protecting the environment has become another criteria for choosing a finish. Shellac stands out as one of the greenest and least toxic coatings available. Shellac is a pure, natural finish that's often used to coat fruits, vegetables and candy. As always, good ventilation and an organic vapor mask are recommended.

Two Keys To Success

1. Thin your shellac to a water-like consistency (Photo 1). A 1 to 1½ lb. cut is ideal for beginners. Pre-mixed shellac is usually a three-pound cut (the exception is Zinnser Bulls Eye Seal Coat, which is a 2 lb. cut). This means three pounds of shellac has been mixed into one gallon of alcohol.

2. Use a high quality brush. A good brush will hold a lot of shellac and apply an even coat without leaving ridges or pronounced brush marks.

One good starter brush is the Winsor & Newton Regency Gold 580 series (Photo 2) made with Taklon synthetic nylon. Another one is the Loew Cornell 7550.

Thin your shellac before use. Store bought shellac is typically a 3 lb. cut. Mix it 1-to-1 with denatured alcohol for a user-friendly 1½ lb. cut.

A 1½ or 2 in. square flat brush made with golden nylon, or "Taklon" bristles is a great starter brush for applying shellac. It's best on flat surfaces but it can handle a cabriole leg with a little practice and it won't break the bank.

Set up a light source at a low angle so it rakes the work area. A raking light will show defects like drips and "holidays" (places you missed) before it's too late to correct them.

Charge the brush by soaking it in denatured alcohol for a few minutes before use. This helps the shellac flow better from the brush.

Brushing Techniques

There are two ways to brush shellac: Lay down a thick layer using a slow gravity-feed method or paint it on thin and work fast. I use both of these brushing techniques on a small tabletop: the gravity-feed method on a molded edge and the rapid-brushing method on a top. I prefer the gravity method on the edges because the brush can cover the whole edge and leave a relatively thick, even coat without worrying about ridges. I use the fast and thin method on the top of the table because it's less prone to leaving ridges and brush marks. For this table I will use a 1½ lb. cut of shellac and a 2 in. Taklon bristle brush.

Set up a raking light so it washes across the area you are brushing (Photo 3). Shellac sets up fast and is pretty unforgiving if a brushing defect goes undetected even for a minute. The light will illuminate any runs and "holidays" (missed spots) before the shellac has time to set. If you notice a brush mark or a holiday, and it's been longer than 10 seconds, leave it alone. Going back will only make it worse. A minor amount of sanding with 320-grit sandpaper will get rid of the brush mark. A holiday will disappear when you apply the next coat.

Charge the brush with some denatured alcohol (Photo 4). Then brush some clean paper to draw out the excess alcohol. Dip your brush into the shellac ¾ of the way up to the ferrule. Hold the brush with your fingers firmly on the ferrule.

When brushing a tabletop, I do the edges first using the gravity feed technique (Photo 5). Don't lay down the shellac so heavy that it forms a run, but do maintain a consistent wet look. End the stroke by exiting off the edge of the table like an airplane taking off. Return to the corner where you began and land your brush in the opposite direction like an airplane touching down (Photo 6). Aim for a few inches inside the wet shellac and run the brush past the corner, taking off as you did in the first stroke.

Work your way around all four edges, taking off and landing as you go. If you should accidentally hit the top, immediately wipe it off with a clean rag.

Switch techniques to brush the flat part of the top and use small rapid strokes to lay down a thin coat. Start the stroke by landing your brush near an edge. Brush on the shellac with a rapid back and forth motion. Shoot for three 10 in. strokes every second. When the brush begins to empty, recharge the brush and land it in the dry area just ahead of where you left off (Photo 7). Do the airplane take-off stroke once you reach the table edge (Photo 8). Don't let the brush hit the edge of the table on a return stroke or you will create a drip for sure. Brush with the grain all the way across the table. On a large surface it is necessary to overlap your strokes (Photo 9). Unlike the gravity feed method that lays down a heavy coat in one continuous motion, this technique lays down a thin layer of shellac with multiple brush strokes. A thin layer sets up fast and does not leave brush marks.

By the time the first coat is done the shellac will be dry enough to apply a second coat. You can take advantage of shellac's fast drying time to apply three coats one

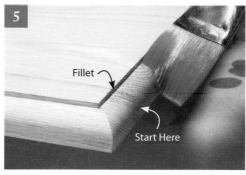

Shellac the edges first. Start the brush stroke an inch or two from the end. Move the brush slowly to lay down a long, consistent wet layer of shellac. Nestle the edge of the brush in the fillet to keep excess shellac from accumulating and running when your back is turned.

Come back to finish the bare spot where you started the stroke. Think of your brush as an airplane. Land the brush near the unfinished end and then lift off right at the edge to avoid snapping the bristles over the edge. Lifting off prevents pools of shellac from being left at the edge and turning into drips.

A completely different brushing technique is used on the top surface. Instead of a long and slow stroke, use short fast strokes. Land the loaded brush in a dry area and with rapid back and forth strokes work the shellac back into the wet area. Aim for a thin, even layer of shellac.

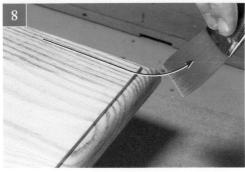

Finish the stroke at the edge. Lift the brush as it passes over the edge just like an airplane taking off. This prevents the brush from pushing shellac over the edge and dripping down the freshly finished edge.

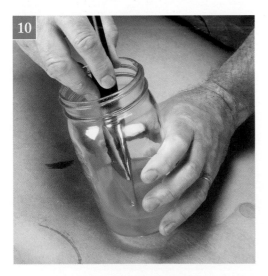

Overlap your strokes on a large surface. Any time you re-wet the brush, land the brush in a dry area. Use a back and forth stroke to blend the new stroke into the wet shellac ahead of it and beside it.

after another with no time for dust to settle in and ruin the finish. With a 1 or 1½ lb. cut of shellac it will take about three coats before you start to develop a noticeable build. I generally try to give the object three light coats for the first setting to seal the wood. I like to lay down a minimum of 9 layers in 3 or more settings for a good build. The time frame for additional coats is dependent on temperature and humidity. If your bristles seem to be dragging while applying another coat, then the previous coat has not yet cured—give it more time to dry. The first setting will leave the surface of the wood rough. A light scuff sanding with some 600-grit sandpaper will remove the whiskers. After that, sanding is not necessary until after the final coat has cured and it's time to rub out the finish.

Allow the shellac to fully cure for a few days. Then, do a final rubout. Shellac can be rubbed out to any sheen you want, high gloss or matte.

With enough practice, you will develop your own preferred blend of shellac and alcohol, your own speed for brushing and your own feel for how wet and thick to lay down the shellac. Eventually, you'll get into the different types of brushes and shellacs that are at your disposal. Trust me, it's a lot of fun.

When the brushing is over, cleaning your brush is a breeze. Just swish it around in a container with clean denatured alcohol. This will clean out most of the shellac from the brush. Unlike varnish or water-based finishes, it okay to leave some residue in the brush.

Pull the brush across a folded paper towel or rag to remove the excess alcohol.

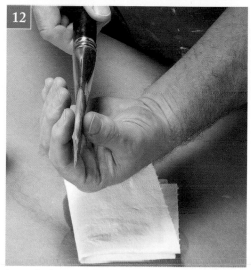

Form the bristles so they dry in their proper shape. The brush will dry stiff from the shellac left in the brush. To use again, just soak the brush in alcohol for a few minutes.

Brush Cleaning

A few sloshes in some clean alcohol will get 95 percent of the shellac out of the brush (Photo 10). Pad the brush with a paper towel or clean rag (Photo 11). Then form the bristles in their proper shape (Photo 12) and you're done. The next time you need to use the brush, place it in some clean alcohol for a few minutes, wipe off the excess on a paper towel and rock and roll.

Finishing with shellac is like any other aspect of woodworking—it takes time and practice to develop the skill. Ultimately, you will find yourself joining the ranks of those who enjoy using a finish that is safe, fully repairable and has a proven historical track record for stability and beauty. That's something really nice to pass on to future generations.

Good luck, and have fun!

FINISHING TIP

Instant Dewaxed Shellac

Take the wax out of shellac and you've got a great sealer that's compatible with most other finishes. It's best to get this "dewaxed" shellac as dry flakes that you mix with denatured alcohol. Usually you have to order the flakes through the mail. But in a pinch, you can decant (draw off one layer of liquid from another) dewaxed shellac from the canned shellac you'll find at the hardware store.

Bring a clean can or lidded jar with you to the store. With the okay of a salesperson, carefully carry a can of shellac to the counter and open it. If the liquid looks creamy, like cappuccino, put the can back and try another one. A good candidate for decanting will contain a clear, deep amber-colored liquid with a creamy-colored layer of residue at the bottom. This indicates that the wax has settled out. You can decant between two and three cups of dewaxed shellac from a quart of liquid shellac. After decanting, pay for the shellac and ask the clerk to dispose of the can with the waxy residue.

Paul Kantor

Decant dewaxed shellac from a can at the hardware store. Find a can in which the wax has settled to the bottom and pour off the pure shellac from the top.

Thin the decanted shellac with an equal amount of denatured alcohol for use as a sealer.

ART DIRECTION: JOEL SPIES • PHOTOGRAPHY: KRIVIT PHOTOGRAPHY • CONSULTANT: MICHAEL DRESDNER

Use Two Brushes to Control Drips

A big brush that holds a lot of finish is great for covering a large flat surface. But that same big brush often leaves too much finish on its thin front edge. The remedy: Use two brushes. First, using the big brush, quickly cover the front edge and an adjacent section of the top with finish. Tip off this swath of finish on the top with the big brush. Then switch to a second smaller brush and smooth out the coat on the edge, removing any sags and drips as you go. Once the edge is finished, switch back to the big brush, feather in where you left off and finish the top.

Drips and sags on the front edge of a board are hard to clean up with a big brush because it leaves a heavy coat that's likely to sag.

Use a second brush—small, disposable foam ones work great—to get rid of drips and sags on edges. The secret is to keep this second brush fairly dry—only dampened with mineral spirits—so it can wick up excess finish. Hold this brush at an angle so it cradles the bottom lip of the edge and make one long end-to-end stroke. If you need to make a second pass, put on a plastic glove and squeeze out the brush with your fingers.

Dry Brush

ART DIRECTION: JOEL SPIES AND DAVID FARR • PHOTOGRAPHY: KRIVIT PHOTOGRAPHY • CONSULTANT: MICHAEL DRESDNER

by RICHARD TENDICK

Not-So-French Polishing

A NEW TWIST ON AN OLD METHOD OF APPLYING SHELLAC

Shellac is the traditional finish on the finest furniture.

You've spent weeks, or months producing that perfect table from a very special wood, and now it's time to apply the finish. What do you reach for? If it's durability you're after, use poly. But if beauty is more important, I'd recommend shellac.

Lacquer can yield equally stunning results, but it's best applied by spraying. Spraying requires specialized equipment and a lot of cleanup with strong solvents. It may not even be legal in states with tough air-quality standards. Shellac is far simpler. All you need is a good brush to apply it and denatured alcohol for cleaning up.

Traditionally, shellac was applied by a process known as French polishing. In this technique, you use a cloth pad to apply dozens of very thin layers of shellac, without sanding between coats. You achieve a high-gloss finish by gradually thinning the shellac. It's very low-tech, but no matter how well you master the technique—and that can take a while—it's a time-consuming process.

EDITOR: TOM CASPAR • PHOTOGRAPHY: JASON ZENTNER

Prepare the surface by sanding up to 220 grit with an orbital sander. Make sure the surface is free of mill marks and scratches by examining it under a raking light.

Sand by hand using 220 grit paper. With a magnifying glass, look for swirl marks left by the orbital sander. Keep sanding until all the swirls are gone.

Today, using a synthetic brush, it's possible to achieve that same build much faster, also without sanding between coats. You achieve the final look—satin or gloss— by using modern abrasives. It's still a shellac finish, but I call it Not-So-French polishing.

Prepare the Surface

Shellac is almost perfectly transparent. It won't obscure flaws, so the wood's surface should be sanded to near-perfection. Fortunately, this rule doesn't usually apply to a whole piece of furniture. It's really only the horizontal surfaces—a top, for example— that require such special treatment. Vertical surfaces such as legs and rails won't reflect light or catch the eye the way a gorgeous top does. You don't have to sand them to the same high standard or apply as many coats of finish as you do for a top.

While there are many ways to make a perfectly smooth surface, the same test applies to each method: Look at the surface under a raking light (Photo 1). The tiny swirls made by a random-orbit sander may not be apparent this way, though, so I go one step further and use a magnifying glass (Photo 2). I figure if it looks good under magnification, it's going to look great without it!

Build the Finish

You can make shellac from flakes and denatured alcohol, but I usually buy cans of premixed Bulls Eye shellac, which is available at most hardware stores. This shellac comes in two shades: clear and amber. I generally use clear shellac on pale woods and amber on dark woods. I've found that thinning premixed shellac with denatured alcohol reduces the size and amount of brush marks so that I don't have to sand between coats. To begin, mix your shellac with an equal amount of alcohol (Photo 3). This thinned mix will keep at least one year, so you can make as much as you want.

Now, a word about brushes. Good ones are worth the money—about $35 for a 2" brush. While you can certainly apply shellac

Thin the shellac with an equal portion of denatured alcohol. On dark woods like walnut, use amber shellac.

Apply the shellac using a high-quality brush to minimize ridges. This brush—my favorite type—has Taklon bristles.

Apply another coat after an hour or so—you don't have to sand. Put on at least twelve coats. Set the top aside to cure for at least one week.

with a cheaper brush, it will leave uneven ridges that require a lot of time to sand out. A good brush leaves a flatter surface. I've used two types of high-quality brushes: badger hair and Taklon (Photo 4). While a badger brush can hold more finish, I think the Taklon is better because it leaves a smoother surface.

Back to the tabletop. First, place it top-face up and brush the edges all around. Some shellac will probably dribble underneath the top; wipe that excess with a rag or your finger. On the top itself, start each brush stroke about 2" from the end of the top, then pull the brush toward that end and off the top. Place the brush back where you started and pull it to the other end. Go back over this wet area with quick back-and-forth strokes to cover any spots you missed and to even out the film. Don't work the shellac too much—it dries very fast. Stop when you start to feel the drag of the drying shellac. Continue this process across the top, overlapping each pass about ¼".

You can recoat the top in an hour or so, but you don't have to clean your brush between coats—one of the benefits of using shellac. When you're done with a coat, just suspend your brush in a jar of denatured alcohol. Hang it so the bristles don't rest on the bottom of the jar and use enough alcohol to completely cover the bristles. Before you apply a new coat, shake out the brush and wipe it a few times on a scrap of wood, then go at it.

Sand with very fine wet/dry paper, using mineral spirits as a lubricant.

Wipe away the slurry and examine the surface. If you see any shiny spots, continue to sand until they're gone.

Recoat the top up to twelve times (Photo 5), or until you get the amount of build you desire. You can take your time; there's no need to do it all in one day.

The bottom side of your top should receive an equal number of coats. You can apply these coats as you go, or wait until you've put the final coat on the top side, then flip the work over and start in on the bottom.

Finish the Finish

Although shellac dries to the touch very fast, much more time is required for it to harden enough to be sanded with fine paper. If you sand too soon, the paper will clog up and the surface will be very uneven. Wait at least one week before smoothing the finish. After this period, you can treat the lower parts of a project differently than the top, just as in sanding and building up coats. Rub these parts with 3/0 or 4/0 steel wool, then follow with a coat of paste wax and buff it out.

A top requires special care. I've found that the best way to smooth the shellac on a top and achieve the final luster, whether satin or gloss, is to sand with wet/dry paper and a lubricant. I use mineral spirits as the lubricant, which requires good ventilation and a respirator, but I'm still looking for something less obnoxious. In any case, you need only work a small area at a time, to minimize the amount of mineral spirits that evaporate.

Start with 600 grit wet/dry paper, wrapped around a rubber, cork or felt sanding block. Squirt a small puddle of mineral spirits onto the surface and start sanding lightly in a circular motion until you create a slurry (Photo 6). Work your way across the surface and apply more mineral spirits as needed. Periodically wipe away the slurry. Let the film of mineral spirits dry, then examine the surface. Sand until the surface has a consistent, dull appearance. If you see any shiny spots (Photo 7), continue to sand until they're gone.

Switch to 1000 grit wet/dry sandpaper and repeat the process. When you wipe away this slurry, the surface will be a bit shinier. Switch to 1500 grit and repeat. The surface will now have a rich, satin appearance. If this is what you want, stop here.

If you want a mirror-like finish, move on to automotive polishes, such as Meguiar's Swirl Remover and Show Car Glaze. Using a soft cloth, squirt a small amount of Swirl Remover on the top and polish with a circular motion (Photo 8). When the top has a consistent shine, switch to Mirror Glaze and repeat.

Shellac is a brittle finish, and scratches easily. To keep scratches to a minimum—particularly on a mirror finish—apply a coat of paste wax.

Use automobile polishes to obtain a higher gloss. You can also use steel wool and wax to create a satin finish.

FINISHING TIP

A Drying Rack for Knobs

In my shop, knobs wet with finish used to be accidents waiting to happen. They'd always end up on the floor. Then I discovered hidden value in a length of triangular scrap: With their fastening screws as counterweights, knobs rest on it securely.

Tim Johnson

ART DIRECTION: VERN JOHNSON • PHOTOGRAPHY: MIKE HABERMANN AND BILL ZUEHLKE

by S. LLOYD NATOF

Brush-On Finish The Easy Way

THINNING THE POLY IS THE SECRET

Finishing is a challenge—right? It's one thing to get a nice finish on a small, flat sample board, but good luck with those inside corners, vertical surfaces, curved areas, thin edges, and framed panels. I don't care for spraying, which comes with its own set of problems, so I've developed a technique to apply a finish by hand, using only a brush and some rags.

The general sequence of steps goes like this: First, I apply a coat or two of thinned-out polyurethane. Then I scuff sand the finish. Finally, I apply a coat of gel varnish to remove the sanding haze. The goal is a finish that appears level and clear, shows the pores and texture of the wood, and feels very smooth.

Applying a finish by hand has many attributes in common with using hand tools. The process is quiet, meditative, and benefits from a methodical approach.

Materials

- **Brush**. I use a 3" foam brush with a wood handle. I cut about 1" off the end of the handle so the brush can be stored in a quart can of finish. This eliminates the use of solvents to clean the brush.
- **Polyurethane**. I use semi-gloss Minwax Fast Drying Polyurethane for the interior of a cabinet and gloss for the outside.
- **Thinner**. I use naphtha rather than paint thinner because it evaporates faster. The goal is to thin the poly so that it will stay wet and flow out better

Brushing a finish is much easier before assembly. For the best results, thin the finish, tape the joints, and lay all the pieces flat on your bench.

EDITOR: DAVE MUNKITTRICK AND TOM CASPAR • PHOTOGRAPHS: MICHAEL HAHN

without extending the drying period too much.

- **Gel varnish**. I like Bartley Gel Varnish.
- **Sandpaper**. I use 3M 216U Fre-Cut Gold stearated sandpaper in P400, P600 and P800 grits.
- **Felt block**. This is for backing the sandpaper.
- **Cotton rags or paper wipes**. I use Brawny medium weight Taskmate Wipers, available at the grocery store.
- **Japan drier**. This helps speed the drying process. It's available at most paint stores.

Technique

I completely pre-finish all the interior surfaces and partially finish the exterior surfaces of a cabinet before assembly. Pre-finishing lets you work on surfaces without having to brush into an inside corner. Pre-finishing also allows you to place all your parts in a horizontal position to prevent drips and runs (Photo 1). You'll finish one surface at a time, letting it dry completely before turning it over to finish the opposite side. Before finishing, tape off mortises, tenons and all glue surfaces with standard masking tape. Trim the tape after it is applied using a utility knife.

Start by sanding everything to 180 grit. Wet the sanded surfaces with a damp rag or sponge. After the wood dries, scuff sand the raised grain using a felt block and 220-grit paper. Wipe off or vacuum the dust. The surface doesn't have to be absolutely dust-free because scuff sanding between coats will smooth out any vagrant dust in

the finish. You won't have to bother with a tack rag.

Next, prepare the finish. Stir ⅓ capful of Japan drier into one quart of poly. Thin the poly with naphtha until it is more like water than syrup (usually about 40% naphtha by volume). The exact amount of thinner is not that important. What you want is a coat that flows out and stays wet while you brush.

Apply the poly using a disposable foam brush. After you're done with each coat, store the brush in a partial can of varnish. One brush will last for all the coats you'll apply.

Working with a foam brush requires some getting used to. The main issues are that it unloads quickly and pushes a small puddle of finish in front of itself. With practice, you will get a sense for the right amount of finish to load into the brush. As for the puddle, let me show you how I finish a large panel.

Start by applying a perimeter of finish roughly 1" from the edge (Photo 2). Then, work the finish back and forth to fill in the middle (Photo 3). To avoid pushing the puddle over the edge of a panel, be sure to keep shy of the edges. Next, work the dry border with a brush that's loaded just enough to wet the wood but not enough to drip over the edge (Photo 4). Go back over the entire surface, in any direction, to move the finish around and create a thin even film with no puddles or dry patches. Finally, brush with the grain using very light strokes at a low angle, like a plane landing (Photo 5). Start the strokes just in from the edge and continue all the way off the opposite

Brushing technique really matters. On a panel, start by brushing a perimeter. Leave a dry border to prevent drips.

Fill in the perimeter. Lay out an even, wet coat of polyurethane over the whole surface, except the border.

Brush the dry border, moving parallel to the edge. Hold the brush lightly, barely overhanging the edge.

Make the final strokes with an unloaded brush, following the grain.

Finish the edges next. Brush on the finish, then wipe it off immediately.

Curved surfaces test your skills. Use a less saturated brush with a light touch and check repeatedly for drips or sags.

end. The only downward pressure should be from the weight of the brush; you are just lightly smoothing the finish in the direction of the grain and don't want to push finish over the edge.

When you're done, examine the panel in a raking light. You should see a wet and even coat of finish. The brush marks should start to flow out and disappear, while the perimeter begins to look drier. If you see puddles or dry spots, move the finish around with the brush. Follow this up with light strokes that go with the grain. Check for drips on the edges and wipe them off.

Next, tackle the edges. Brush on the poly and wipe it off right away with a cloth (Photo 6). This leaves a thin film of varnish that won't sag or drip. It's enough protection for edges that won't be handled very often. Use a raking light to check for a ridge of finish that may have been pushed onto the top. If you see one, smooth it out with a light brush stroke following the grain.

If you want to have more finish on an edge, wait until the faces are dry, then stand the part up on edge for brushing. Don't forget to wipe off any drips after brushing the edges.

If you're finishing a curved part, use a much drier brush (Photo 7). Dip the brush's tip in the finish and stroke lightly with the brush held in a vertical position. Limit your working area to one face and brush out a thin, even coat. Wipe off the adjacent faces to remove any drips.

When you're done brushing, clean the can's rim, drop in the brush, hold a deep breath for a minute, and exhale into the can. Quickly put on the lid. This helps to replace the oxygen in the can with carbon dioxide, which minimizes the skin that may develop on the finish's surface.

Lightly scuff sand every surface after it has dried for one day (Photo 8). Be careful near the edges, where the finish can be extra-thin. The edges that you wiped off should already be smooth, but if you need to sand out a little fuzz, use a very light touch with 800-grit paper.

Once you're done sanding, use a new foam brush to apply 2-3 coats of gel varnish to the interior surfaces only (Photo 9). Working one part at a time, brush the gel on most of the surface, then smear it around and begin to remove it with a wipe in each hand. Switch to a new set of wipes to remove all the excess gel varnish (Photo 10). Any remaining gel will dry to a sticky mess, so get it off now. Use a clean, folded wipe on the edges. Remove any vagrant gel from the underside of the part and clean off smudges from your hands on the top.

Now you can remove the tape and glue your project together. Apply two coats of thin gloss poly on the outside surfaces (Photo 11). Sand with 400 grit in between coats. If you're finishing a cabinet, brush one side at a time, rotating the case to bring a new side horizontal after the previous side has dried. You should be able to finish two or three sides in one day. Blankets and padding are important to protect the sides from damage as you rotate the cabinet. Wipe off any drips that may form on the edges (Photo 12).

Scuff sand with 400-grit sandpaper after the first coat has dried overnight. Wrap the paper around a felt block.

Apply gel varnish to all the interior parts with a foam brush. Gel varnish helps remove the sanding haze.

Wipe off all the gel with two rags and two hands. Remove the tape from the joints, then glue and assemble your project.

Apply a second coat of poly to the outside of the project.

Wipe up any drips that form on the edges with a folded towel.

Light-Sanding Zone

Sand the exterior surfaces with 600-grit paper. Sand to within ⅛" of an edge, then make very light passes in this zone.

Note: The used wipes should be spread out to dry when you are done.

Wait at least two days for the second coat to dry. Then lightly scuff sand with 600-grit paper to dull the glossy surface by about one-third (Photo 13). Repeat with 800-grit paper wrapped around the felt block. This time, push down harder to level the surface (Photo 14). Look for a 90% sanded surface with an even pattern of small, shiny pores after you wipe off the dust.

Finally, use a gel varnish to reduce the sanding haze, just as you did with the interior surfaces (Photo 15). I usually apply two to five coats of gel on top of the poly to get the finish I am looking for. For my really special pieces and on dark finishes, I polish with 3M's Imperial Hand Glaze #5990 between the last coats of gel. I rarely use wax except on thin or satin finishes.

This finishing process can be used over dyes and stains, but you must be very careful near the edges, especially with dyes. Dark colors require more coats of gel and Hand Glaze polishing to remove the sanding haze.

Repeat the process using 800-grit paper to level the surface. Again, sand much less near the edges.

Apply gel varnish until you get the look you're after.

by ERIC SMITH

Super-Smooth Poly Finish

A DEFECT-FREE FINISH, EVEN WITH A BRUSH

Polyurethane is a tough, high-quality finish, ideal for tabletops and other surfaces that take a lot of abuse. But no matter how clean your finishing area or how good your brushing technique, a few bubbles, dust particles and streaky spots always manage to sneak into the final coat (Photo 1, next page). Directions on the can don't say anything about it— leaving you to assume a less-than-perfect finish must be your own fault. However, the solution is quite simple—rub out the finish with fine sandpaper and synthetic steel wool. Sanding removes defects and levels ridges. Synthetic steel wool creates an even, silky smooth finish that's a joy to look at and feel. This age-old two-step technique is commonly used on shellac and lacquer finishes, but it can work well on water- and oil-based polyurethane, too. The only drawback with poly is that it is difficult to bring up to a high gloss. If a satin or semi-gloss look is what you're after, this technique will give you great results.

Polyurethane varnish is the most durable finish for tabletops.

EDITOR: DAVE MUNKITTRICK • ART DIRECTION AND PHOTOGRAPHY: VERN JOHNSON

Materials and Supplies

Sandpaper

Sandpaper is used to flatten the finish and remove dust nibs and brush marks. Stearated aluminum-oxide sandpaper is by far the best product for sanding a finish. Stearated paper has dry lubricants that help prevent "corning" or the balling up of finish on the paper. Wet-dry silicon-carbide paper balls up like crazy if you don't use water as a lubricant. The trouble with wet sanding is the water slurry can make it difficult to see your progress.

Synthetic Steel Wool

I used synthetic steel wool on both water- and oil-based polyurethane. Traditional steel wool is not recommended for water-based finishes; it sheds steel particles that leave a mess and give the user steel wool slivers. Synthetic steel wool pads equivalent to 00 steel wool are widely available at home centers and hardware stores. Fine synthetic wool equivalent to 0000 steel wool is harder to find. I had good luck at auto-body supply stores and mail-order wood-working suppliers.

Powdered Abrasives

Pumice and rottenstone are sold at some paint stores and at woodworking suppliers. Pumice is ground volcanic glass that comes in grades from 1F (coarse) to 4F (fine). Rottenstone is even finer than 4F pumice. It's made of ground limestone.

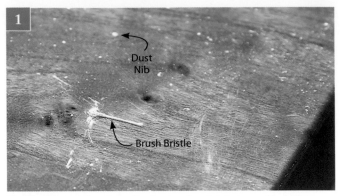

The Problem: A few dust nibs, broken brush bristles and bubbles are almost inevitable on big horizontal surfaces finished with slow-drying polyurethane.

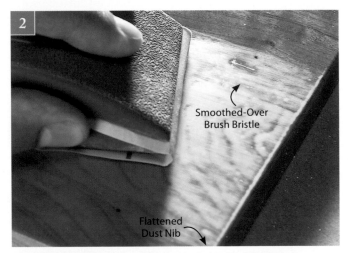

The Solution: Flatten the surface imperfections with 600-grit sandpaper on a sanding block (or 400-grit followed by 600 if the surface is really a mess). Sand just enough to flatten bubbles, dust nibs and ridges, but don't try to sand away all the shiny spots.

Build a Good Foundation for the Finish

1. I use 220-grit sandpaper for final sanding on raw wood. I always sand a little bit longer than I think is necessary. Then I vacuum thoroughly and wipe the wood with a clean, soft cloth until I stop getting dust on my fingers when I run them over the wood.

2. Use grain filler on open-pored woods, such as oak or walnut. Otherwise after rubbing out, the pores will look shiny compared with the rest of the wood.

3. Before applying finish on any project, test different finishing options on scrap pieces of wood. Water- and oil-based polyurethane finishes look completely different. If the color doesn't look right or seems too bland, which is sometimes a problem with water-based finishes, use a sealer coat of clear, wax-free shellac or experiment with stains to warm the color of the wood before applying the topcoats.

4. I applied a gloss polyurethane on my tabletop because it can be rubbed to any sheen from flat to semi-gloss. I used a semi-gloss poly on the rest of the table. Vertical surfaces and legs don't collect the dust the way a flat, horizontal top does. A light buffing with steel wool will clean the occasional dust nib on vertical surfaces.

5. Sand with 320- to 400-grit stearated paper between coats, depending on how smooth the coat looks. Use a sanding block to level ridges and bumps. With a gloss finish, coarser paper may leave scratches that are visible through subsequent layers of poly.

6. Apply an extra coat or two of polyurethane on tabletops for more durability, depth and protection. Lay the last coat on a little thick to protect against accidentally rubbing through the top layer of finish. Remember, polyurethane does not melt into itself the way shellac or lacquer do. Each layer sits on top of the previous one, so there is a danger of sanding through one layer into the next. This will leave a visible ghost line where the top layer was sanded through. If this happens, you need to reapply the last layer of polyurethane and start over.

7. Finish the test boards at the same time you're finishing your tabletop. Use these sample pieces to make sure the finish is properly cured and ready to rub out. Then experiment on them to get a feel for rubbing out.

8. Let the finish fully cure! This is most important for a successful rubout. A finish that has not cured will not be hard enough to take an even scratch pattern from abrasives. The result will be an uneven sheen. Polyurethane should cure for two weeks to a month after the last coat is applied. If the finish balls up on the sandpaper or it won't buff out to more than a satin sheen, let it sit for another week or two.

Smooth and Flatten the Finish

It seems completely counterintuitive, but to make a finish really shine, you have to start by sanding it dull (Photo 2). Sanding removes dust nibs and brush marks and leaves the finish smooth and flat.

Caution: Finish tends to be thinner at tabletop edges. Use special care in these areas to avoid sanding through (Photo 3).

9. Apply consistent, light pressure as you sand. When you're done, the surface should feel smooth and level and will still have a few small shiny spots. Don't feel that you have to completely erase

every visual defect at this point—just go for a smooth feel. Unless you have lots of bubbles to flatten, you should only need to sand five to 10 strokes in any given area with the 600-grit sandpaper. Sand dry so you can see what's happening to the finish, and change paper often. Vacuum all the sanding dust off the surface and wipe with a damp cloth. Tackcloths can be used on oil-based poly but not on water-based.

Rub to an Even, Flat Sheen

10. Begin rubbing-out with medium-grade, (00 steel wool equivalent) synthetic abrasive pads (Photo 4). This is where the finish begins to come to life, taking on an attractive, flat sheen with no visible defects.

Rub to a Satin Sheen

11. Clean the top with a damp cloth and continue buffing with fine synthetic abrasive wool (0000 steel wool equivalent) (Photo 5). Rub until the whole piece has an even, satiny sheen, and then rub a little more. There's not much danger of rubbing through the finish at this point.

Extra care should be taken when sanding near the edges of a tabletop to avoid sanding through. Sand the 2 to 3 in. nearest the edge first. Short strokes make it easier to control the block. After the edges are done, sand the centers with long strokes that overlap the sanded border.

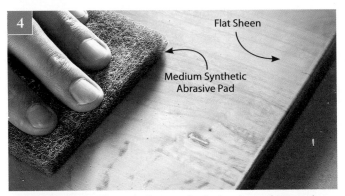

Rub out the finish using a medium synthetic abrasive pad (00 steel wool equivalent). Rub until you get a flat, even sheen across the entire surface.

Switch to a fine synthetic abrasive wool (0000 steel wool equivalent) to bring the finish to a satin sheen.

For a semi-gloss sheen, continue rubbing with fine synthetic abrasive wool lubricated with soapy water.

Rottenstone

Using finer and finer abrasives brings the sheen closer to a full gloss. Start with finest-grade (4F) pumice lubricated with water and a moist rag, followed by rottenstone. With these finer grits, it's OK to use a circular motion as you rub.

Rub to a Semi-Gloss

12. To bring up the sheen even more, use soapy water or paraffin oil as a lubricant for the abrasive wool (Photo 6). Rub thoroughly; then wipe dry.

13. If that's still not enough shine for you, rub the entire surface with 4F-grade pumice. After sprinkling the pumice on the surface, rub it into a paste with water and a dampened rag (Photo 7). Wipe the slurry away, and then repeat the process with rottenstone. Keep firm pressure on the rag, and sprinkle more of the powder or water as needed. Continue rubbing in any direction until your arms hurt and the finish looks satisfactory. Now your furniture has the good-looking finish it deserves.

Dealing with Molded Edges

Avoid using sandpaper on molded edges, table legs and other vertical surfaces. The risk of cutting through the finish with the sandpaper is just too great. Instead, rub molded edges with synthetic abrasive pads and rub to the sheen of the top.

by MICHAEL DRESDNER

Put Down Your Brush!

IT'S NOT ALWAYS THE BEST TOOL FOR THE JOB

For most of us, when it comes to finishing, the goal is to get the stuff on the surface as quickly and easily as possible. Traditionalists may argue that once you learn how to use them, brushes are the most versatile and efficient tools for applying finishes. I say, brushing is not always best.

Flooding and wiping offers several advantages over brushing. Each coat is

Using a rag takes no training at all. And nothing is quite as rewarding as wiping finish onto your carefully prepared surface and seeing the wood come to life.

of uniform thickness, so it'll dry quickly and evenly. Dust can't settle in it because the layer of finish is so thin. And even though you'll have to apply more coats, you don't have to sand in between, there's no technique to learn and no brush to clean.

Oil stains and Danish oil finishes are designed to be flooded on and wiped (Photo 1). I've found this is a great approach for lots of other finishing chores, including raising the grain before finishing (Photo 2) and applying water-soluble dyes and stains (Photo 3). I always apply my seal coat of dewaxed shellac with a rag (Photo 4). Some oil varnishes are formulated at the factory for wiping, but most brush-on types can also be applied this way, if you thin them first with boiled linseed oil (one cup to a quart of varnish).

How to Flood the Surface

The idea is to flood the wood with finish, let it drink up as much as it can, then wipe off the excess. Immersing the entire piece in a bath of finish is usually not

Raise the grain before you apply any water-based finish by liberally wetting the sanded wood with a sponge. After wetting, squeeze out the sponge and soak up any excess water immediately, leaving the surface damp. This quick wetting won't affect glue joints or loosen veneer. After overnight drying, sand lightly before applying the finish.

Spray water-soluble stains and dyes from bottles. It's a quick and easy way to cover large or vertical surfaces and keep them from drying out. Wet the entire surface with water first. Then spray on the color, working from the bottom up. After you've got the surface flooded, wipe it down evenly with a rag. You can put oil-based stains on this way too, although they don't atomize as well and cleaning the spray bottle afterward is a chore.

practical, and pouring stain directly on the surface can result in unsightly dark spots. Used with a rag, a spray bottle ($2) is a great way to cover a surface quickly, but all you really need is a rag. A good rag allows you to get finish onto the surface cleanly and recoat porous areas easily.

What Makes a Good Rag?

Absorbency and a tight weave. Whether transferring material from the can to the surface or soaking up the excess while evening out the coat, a rag that can hold a lot of liquid works the best. Loosely woven rags shed tiny threads of fabric (lint) that contaminate surfaces. For applying oils, shellac and varnishes, the best rags come from all-cotton fabrics—old towels, diapers, tee shirts—the softer the better. You can

also buy cotton rags from finishing suppliers. Paper towels may be a convenient substitute, but cheap ones leave lint and disintegrate quickly. I prefer "shop wipes," a thicker, more durable and absorbent type of paper towel. They're available at home centers, are virtually lint-free and only cost about five cents apiece.

Sponges are another useful alternative because they're so absorbent. They hold lots of water or thin, runny stains without dripping, so you can flood and wipe a large surface quickly and cleanly.

Dispose of Oily Rags Safely

After use, rags, wipes and sponges saturated with oils from finishing products are a serious fire hazard. These oils—boiled linseed and tung oil are most common—dry to a film when exposed to air. This drying process can generate enough heat to cause a pile of wet, oil-soaked rags to spontaneously catch on fire within a few hours. Dry these rags safely (Photo 5) before throwing them out and keep them out of the reach of children and pets.

For safety, spread out oil-soaked rags, one layer thick, so air can circulate around them. This allows the heat generated by the oils as they dry to dissipate so the rags won't spontaneously catch on fire. Once dry, they'll be hard and crusty, and can be safely tossed into the household trash.

FINISHING TIP

The Perfect Pad for Water-based Poly

Remember finger painting in kindergarten? Wouldn't it be great if finishing could be that fun and easy? It can be with paint pad sponges. No more tortured hand positions as you maneuver a brush handle around chair rungs or into panel corners. These soft pads conform to contours while the short nylon bristles lay down an even coat of finish. The ends are cut at an angle so getting into corners is a breeze. The sponges also hold a lot of material, which means fewer trips back to the pan when finishing a large, flat surface. Look for pad sponges in the paint department of home centers and hardware stores.
Dave Munkittrick

Nylon Bristles

ART DIRECTION: JOEL SPIES • PHOTOGRAPHY: KRIVIT PHOTOGRAPHY • CONSULTANT: MICHAEL DRESDNER

FINISHING TIP

Warm the Look of Water-based Polyurethane

Water-based polyurethane finishes often make wood look parched (at right, top). Because they don't change the wood's color the way oil-based finishes do, the wood still looks raw. Tinting water-based poly with amber-colored dye adds the warm color that's missing (at right, bottom).

It's easy. You can use either water- or alcohol-based dye. The dye is available as a dry powder or pre-mixed. If you choose the powder, mix it with water or alcohol following the instructions on the package. Add a teaspoon of the mixture to a quart of finish. Never add dry powder directly to the polyurethane. If you use a premixed liquid concentrate, add about five drops to a quart of poly. Experiment on scrap to get the right color intensity. Just remember—you'll want to apply three or four coats of water-based poly for adequate protection, and each tinted coat will add a little color, so use the dye sparingly.

Adding color this way has another big advantage—it's blotch-free. Unlike stains, which can cause blotches when they soak in, water-based poly forms a film on top of the surface. No soak, no blotch.

Kelly Schrenk

Clear Water-based Poly

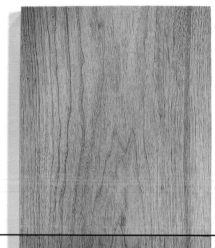

Tinted Water-based Poly

ART DIRECTION: JOEL SPIES • PHOTOGRAPHY: KRIVIT PHOTOGRAPHY • CONSULTANT: MICHAEL DRESDNER

by TIM JOHNSON

Brush a Tabletop

GET GREAT RESULTS WITHOUT RUBBING OUT

Maybe I'm crazy, but I like to brush polyurethane. I've built more than 50 dining room tables, and I've brush-finished every one, using a simple system that consistently provides great results.

I'm not a purist. I use tools that you can get at any paint store and I don't rub out the final coat. My tabletop finishes look good and feel smooth. They're durable...and do-able.

A tabletop requires multiple coats, of course, but each one is applied the same way. I use flat, satin or semi-gloss

Use gravity to help fight brush marks. A single spacer allows positioning your top at a slight angle, to help the polyurethane flow.

polyurethane, depending on the look I want and the wood. A lower sheen helps to disguise finish imperfections, but it can make dark woods such as walnut look a bit hazy.

You can practice my methods by finishing the bottom of your tabletop. It should have at least one coat of finish anyway, to stabilize the top for seasonal changes in humidity.

Set Up for Success

I always sand with 280-grit paper between finish coats, and I let the polyurethane dry thoroughly before sanding. I wipe the top twice to remove the sanding dust, first with a slightly damp lint-free cloth, then with a fresh tack cloth.

After final sanding, I vacuum the top thoroughly before moving it into my finishing area. I like to apply finishes early in the morning, when the air is still and airborne debris has had all night to settle.

I always slope tabletops for finishing (Photo 1). Taking this step helps me

Top-Brushing Trio

My brush arsenal for tabletops includes a 2½-in. bristle brush for the top's wide, flat surface, a 2-in. foam brush for its long edges and a 3-in. trim roller for the ends.

Choose a natural-bristle brush for oil-based polyurethane. Its business end should appear wedge-shaped or tapered when viewed from the side. Most natural bristle brushes are made with Chinese hog bristles. China bristles, as they're called, are relatively large. I prefer brushes that combine china bristles and ox hair. Ox hair is finer than china bristle (and more expensive), so it's less likely to leave marks. The tips of china bristles are often flagged (split into multiple fibers) to imitate ox hair. I like long, flat wooden handles. They're comfortable to hold and offer good balance. A stainless-steel ferule won't rust—a must for any brush you plan to keep long-term. The "Demon" flat sash brush from Bestt Liebco and the Purdy "Ox-O-Thin" are good, reasonably-priced brushes for oil-based polyurethane.

Set up a low-angle light to highlight imperfections. Use its sharp contrast to spot wayward brush strokes, loose bristles and other debris that appears in the finish.

Wipe the surface with a tack rag after vacuuming. I never vacuum in my finishing area, though, because the vac's exhaust stirs up the air.

think positively about the job ahead, because it makes me feel like I'm doing everything possible to insure a good outcome.

A low-angle light creates shadows that make it easy to see imperfections in the finish (see Photo 2). I use this light immediately, to check for debris missed by the tack rag (Photo 3).

Prime and Stir

Natural bristle brushes work best when the bristles are saturated with solvent (Photo 4).

Saturated bristles release the polyurethane efficiently and make the brush easier to clean.

Thoroughly stir the polyurethane. Then pour enough to complete the job into a separate container (Photo 5). I always open a new can of polyurethane for the final coat.

My secret weapon against brush marks is Penetrol (Photo 6). Penetrol makes brushing easier, whether it's hot, humid, cold or dry. (Polyurethane is usually formulated to perform best at 70-degrees F. and 50-percent relative humidity—when do you ever finish in those conditions?) Adding mineral spirits also makes polyurethane easier to brush, but it thins the finish, so you might have to apply more coats. Adding Penetrol doesn't thin the finish. I usually start by adding two capfuls per pint of polyurethane. Like mineral spirits, Penetrol slows the drying time, which increases the chances of accumulating dust in the finish.

Brush and Roll

Before I brush the top, I prime the end grain (Photo 7). This method prevents ugly drip marks that can result when you brush the top first, because drips that soak into unfinished end grain create permanent marks.

Rather than brushing the top's entire surface, I divide it into sections that are easier to manage. For each section, brushing on the polyurethane is a two-step process.

First I flow it on (Photo 8). Then I brush it out (Photo 9).

I load the brush by dipping it ⅓ of the way into the polyurethane. Then, starting on the top's low side, I go directly to the surface, without tapping the brush on the sides of the measuring cup. Just dip and go, man. I apply the polyurethane liberally and reload my brush often. While coating this first section of the top, I also include its adjacent long edge.

About the only mistake you can make during this step is being too stingy with the polyurethane. Covering the surface quickly and uniformly is most important. Brushing direction doesn't matter, except at the ends. There I brush parallel to the edges, to apply the polyurethane evenly and minimize drips.

After using the low-angle light to make sure the section is completely covered, I level the polyurethane with end-to-end strokes. The brush wicks up excess finish during this process, so before each stroke, I unload

Removing Debris

Inevitably, dust, hair, bristles or bugs will lodge in the wet finish. I use the edge of the brush to lift them off the surface as soon as I see them—it's too late if the poly has started to set up. After removing the offender, I brush lightly end-to-end to eliminate pock marks left by the process.

Prime your brush by soaking it in solvent for a few minutes. The solvent saturates the porous natural bristles, so they don't soak up the polyurethane and become tacky. Suspend the brush so its bristles don't rest on the bottom of the glass.

Pour enough polyurethane to complete the job into a clean container. I use a plastic measuring cup. It's light in weight, easy to hold and the wide opening allows plenty of room for the brush.

Make polyurethane easier to brush by adding Penetrol, a conditioner for oil based paint and varnish. Penetrol extends the open time, increases flowablilty and improves leveling, all without thinning the finish.

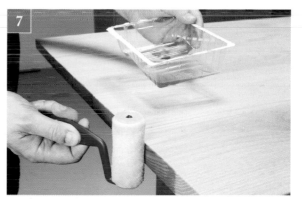

Start finishing the top by priming the end grain, so drips from brushing the top won't leave permanent marks. A trim roller quickly applies an even, drip-free coat of polyurethane.

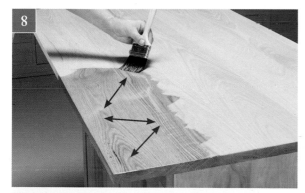

Finish the top in stages. Brush on the polyurethane in sections that are about 12-in.-wide. Your goals are to cover each section quickly and uniformly, using a minimum number of brush stokes. Brushing diagonally across the grain helps to evenly spread the polyurethane.

Brush end-to-end to level the finish and align the brush marks with the grain. Make as few strokes as possible. Over-brushing leaves visible brush marks.

the brush by gently pressing it inside the measuring cup's rim. I use an especially light touch at the beginning of each stroke, to avoid leaving a pool of varnish.

I don't brush out the last couple inches of the section, because I'll be brushing back into this portion later. When the raking light shows that all the brush marks run with the grain, I switch to a dry foam brush to clean the adjacent long edge (Photo 10). Most bristle brushes deposit too much polyurethane for this job, creating as many drips and sags as they remove.

I move to the other side of the table to brush the next section, so I'm not leaning over the wet finish (Photo 11). I cut back into the wet polyurethane as soon as possible. The longer it sets up, the more likely it is to show brush marks. I check my work in the raking light before moving on to the last section, and then again when that section—including its adjacent long edge—is completed.

When the top looks good in raking light, I complete the job by cleaning the ends with the roller and dry foam brush (Photo 12). Then I walk away. Experience has taught me to leave tiny imperfections. They look bad when the varnish is wet, but they virtually disappear when the varnish is dry.

Switch to a dry foam brush to clean the front edge. It soaks up drips and sags and leaves a thin, even coat. Clean the edge of the bottom, too.

Cover the adjacent section with polyurethane. Brush back into the wet area you've just completed to tie the two sections together. Follow with light end-to-end strokes as before. Repeat the process to finish the top.

Remove drips from the ends. The roller re-wets the polyurethane and amalgamates the drips. Follow with the foam brush to level the finish.

by KEVIN SOUTHWICK

Wipe-On / Rub-Off Finishing

THIS TWO-STEP PROCESS GUARANTEES FLAWLESS RESULTS

No brush marks, drips, runs, bubbles, hairs, dust or orange peel—and beautiful results every time. For most furniture projects, it doesn't get easier than using a wipe-on/rub-off finishing process. This two-step method eliminates all the usual problems because rubbing off all of the finish that isn't absorbed by the wood leaves no wet film in which the problems can occur. The clear and important difference between this method and all others (including wiping on and leaving a film build) is the rubbing off. No attempt is made to build a film on the surface of the wood. Rubbing off the source of all the problems is the big trick.

The wipe-on/rub-off method avoids time spent cleaning brushes and it dramatically reduces or eliminates sanding between coats. There are some limitations, though. This method can produce only a satin to semi-gloss finish and the finish itself won't be waterproof (see "One Drawback," page 64).

Finishes suitable or formulated for wiping on and rubbing off are widely available. They offer convenience, but you can also easily concoct your own wipe-on/rub-off finish. Thinning out an oil-based brushing varnish is one way. In fact, just about any finish can be wiped on and rubbed off, as long as it doesn't dry too fast. Shellac, lacquer and most water-based finishes fall into this category; they get sticky before you can rub them off.

Some finishes can be thinned and wiped on—with no brushwork at all.

Make your own high-quality wipe-on/rub-off finish by blending 100% pure tung oil, boiled linseed oil and polyurethane varnish.

Finish-sand to a finer grit than for a film-building finish. Wipe-on/rub-off finish shows scratches that a built-up finish hides.

Rub in the wet finish to create a silky-smooth surface.

Keep wiping until your last rag comes up clean.

Choosing the right material(s) for your wipe-on/rub-off finish can be confusing. Tung oil and linseed oil are natural vegetable oils that have been in use for ages. Paste wax is another classic wipe-on/rub-off finish. Then there are products like gel varnish, "Danish oil" and wiping varnish, as well as custom blends you can mix up yourself. So how do you choose the right formula? Here are three simple considerations.

■ The type of resin (or solids). The materials that remain and harden to seal the wood after the solvents evaporate are important because they have varying degrees of amber tone, working time and durability. For example, boiled linseed oil has more amber color than pure tung oil, while pure tung oil has a longer working time. Oil-based varnishes come in a variety of tones, will dry much faster and are more durable in every way than both tung oil and linseed oil.

- The thickness of the material. Thicker or more concentrated material is more effective at sealing the wood, but may be harder to apply and remove. For example, brushing varnish straight from the can is hard to rub off because it's thick and goopy. Rubbing off is much easier if the varnish is thinned out.
- Working time and drying time. Faster drying time means less working time, so it's important to choose a material that has enough working time to allow you to get it all rubbed off before it gets sticky. You'll need a long working time if you plan to rub in the finish with wet/dry sandpaper. Products with a lot of oils have the longest working time—they require a day or longer to properly cure. Gel varnish, on the other hand, dries so fast you can apply two coats in one day.

One favorite wipe-on/rub-off finish is a combination of equal parts boiled linseed oil, 100% pure tung oil, and polyurethane varnish (Photo 1). This blend balances the color and drying time of the two oils and is more durable due to the addition of the polyurethane. You can thin the blend to make it easier to smear around and remove. Use a gloss poly varnish to slightly increase the sheen. Master furniture maker Sam Maloof used this type of finish extensively. He even developed his own branded version, which you can find on the Internet. To make a "Danish oil"-type material, simply thin any oil-based brushing varnish 50% or more with mineral spirits or paint thinner.

Tips for Applying

- When you prep the bare wood for a wipe-on/rub-off finish, sand to a higher grit than you would for a film building finish (220-400 grit vs. 150 grit, Photo 2). The quality of the sheen of a wipe-on/rub-off finish is determined by the smoothness or texture of the wood surface itself. The 150 grit scratches that would be filled by the layers of a film-building finish will leave the wipe-on/rub-off surface looking dull and lifeless.
- If you choose a finishing material that has enough working time you can create a surface that looks spectacular and feels super-smooth by rubbing in the first application of finish (Photo 3). Use a soft block and fine wet/dry sandpaper (600-1000 grit) to create a slurry that helps to seal the wood. You can feel the difference immediately by running your finger across the still-wet wood. This step needs to be done only once, unless you miss a spot. Following this application, two more wipe-on/rub-off coats are usually enough to create a nice finish; more coats will slightly increase the sheen.
- The best way to determine if you've removed all of the finish that hasn't been absorbed by the wood is to continue rubbing with clean rags until they remain completely dry, showing no signs of excess finish (Photo 4). Good rags for this process are soft and absorbent; knit cotton and Scott shop towels are good choices. Note: The finish-soaked rags are likely to spontaneously combust, so spread them flat out-of-doors to dry hard.

■ Only two problems commonly occur with wipe-on/rub-off finishes and they're both easily avoided. The first occurs when wet finish that isn't absorbed by the wood is left on the surface to create streaks, rag marks, and sticky or shiny spots. The second occurs as slower-drying oils or excess solvents bleed back out of the pores of the wood and leave little rings. If they're still wet, these rings can be removed by rubbing. But if they're allowed to harden on the surface, they must be sanded off.

One Drawback— It's Not Waterproof

It's virtually impossible to achieve a 100% waterproof seal with a wipe-on/rub-off finish alone. Fortunately, there's an easy fix: Just apply a thin coat of waterproof material on top. That's all it takes to build a consistent, durable film. In fact, if you want a waterproof coating that retains the low sheen and very "close to the wood" look of an oil finish, the wipe-on/rub-off method is an excellent and thorough way to prep the wood's surface.

After three rounds of wipe-on/rub-off finish on the entire piece, brush one coat of thinned-out (25–50%) oil-based brushing varnish on the top or any other horizontal surface that a glass or cup might find. Don't bother to brush vertical surfaces—there's really no need to make them waterproof.

If brushing creates a dust or brush-mark problem, you don't have to wait until the next day to deal with it. Simply wash off the messed-up varnish film with paint thinner or mineral spirits and try again. Most oil-based products can be removed this way for at least an hour or more.

Strain Your Varnish

Have you ever tried to use varnish from a skinned over, half-used can? Even if you remove the skin carefully, lumps of dried finish get mixed in with the remaining varnish and eventually end up on your project. But don't throw the stuff away—there's an easy way to get clean varnish from a used can. Just pour the contents through a paint filter into a second container. The filter is a paper cone with a cheesecloth nose (available at paint stores and home centers). Working from a second container is a good idea anyway—it keeps the storage can from getting messed up. The brush often transfers bits of junk it picks up from the surface back to the container, so clean the leftovers again when you pour them back into the storage can. You can use the same filter if it hasn't dried out.

Tim Johnson

Disposing of Mineral Spirits

Most of us don't think twice about tossing out small amounts of mineral spirits. We should, however, because mineral spirits release smog-producing and ozone-destroying volatile organic compounds (VOCs) when they evaporate. Small amounts of mineral spirits tossed out by individual woodworkers (there are over 17 million of us in the U.S.!) add up. The EPA recommends that all used mineral spirits be disposed of at a hazardous waste collection facility. For professional woodworkers and finishers, the transportation and disposal of mineral spirits and other solvent wastes may be regulated. Check with the appropriate state agency.

ART DIRECTION: VERN JOHNSON • PHOTOGRAPHY: MIKE HABERMANN AND BILL ZUEHLKE • CONSULTANTS: MICHAEL DRESDNER AND JUDY KLEIMAN, REGION 5 EPA

by KEVIN SOUTHWICK

Finish an Exterior Door

HOW TO CHOOSE AND APPLY A LONG-LASTING CLEAR FINISH

EDITOR: TIM JOHNSON • PHOTOGRAPHY: JASON ZENTNER

What do fancy wooden boats and beautiful wooden front doors have in common? They both need a clear finish that can really stand up to the elements. Sunlight, water, extreme temperature changes and abrasions are bound to occur in both situations. Most clear coatings just can't take that type of abuse and will fail in a year or two, allowing discoloration and damage to the wood.

Clear Exterior Varnishes

Spar varnishes are formulated to be resilient under outdoor conditions. They're more elastic than regular varnish, so they're less likely to crack as the wood continuously expands and contracts with changing outdoor conditions. Some spar varnishes also contain very effective UV inhibitors. The finishes with the best track record for exterior use come from the marine industry, where spar varnish originated.

Spar varnishes are usually glossy. A glossy sheen looks good on a wooden boat and also tells the owner when it's time to apply a fresh coat of finish. A loss of sheen indicates that the finish is beginning to degrade and it's time for recoating. Some brands offer a lower

Dowels suspend the door so the entire surface can be coated with marine spar varnish.

sheen option, usually recommended for application as the topcoat over several coats of high gloss for the best results.

Most of the spar varnishes at hardware and paint stores will work well on an exterior door that's tucked under a front porch, where the sun and rain are kept at a distance. But for a door that will be fully exposed year round in a harsh climate, a high-quality oil-based marine-grade spar varnish will provide both good looks and a long service life before it requires maintenance.

Tung oil and phenolic resin are the key ingredients in many marine-grade spar varnishes. The most technically advanced marine spar varnish formulations also contain ultra violet (UV) light inhibitors. UV inhibitors reduce the effect of the sun's rays by changing UV light energy to heat, which can then dissipate without harming the finish or the wood beneath it. These are expensive ingredients and are reflected in the cost. A quart of the good stuff is expensive, but this is a small price to pay compared to a finish that fails after a year or two.

Unfortunately, it's almost always impossible to identify the ingredients by reading the label (or even the Material Safety Data Sheet), because they're rarely listed. Some brands do list ingredients on their websites or other literature. Be aware that labels can carry misleading claims, such as "maximum UV protection" or "UV stabilized," even though the product doesn't contain any significant UV inhibitors. That's why the spar varnishes that I trust the most are specifically designed for and tested over time in the most extreme conditions. These premium spar varnishes are also formulated to level well (reducing brush marks) and to allow ample working time. Finding such spar varnishes usually requires shopping at a marine supply store or in the advertising pages or websites of boating magazines.

Applying Spar Varnish

I'll start by preparing this new entry door for finishing by wetting it to eliminate hidden marks (Photo 1), sanding it to remove unsightly factory sanding marks (Photo 2) and standing it, so both sides and all the edges can be finished at the same time (Photos 3 and 4).

Next, I'll apply a dark brown oil-based pigmented stain (Photo 5). Pigmented stain adds more than color—the pigments provide some UV protection for the wood as well. When the stain is thoroughly dry, I'll apply three coats of Epifanes clear high gloss varnish—my favorite premium marine spar varnish (Photo 6). To give the door a hand-rubbed appearance, I'll switch to Epifanes wood finish matte for the final coat. This finish—five layers all told—will provide many years of protection before requiring maintenance.

I'll use a 2" natural bristle varnish brush and small round sash brushes to apply the varnish. The 2" brush will do the bulk of the surface (Photos 7–10); the sash brushes provide better control on the moldings around the raised panels (Photo 11). They're also the best tools for removing drips (Photo 12). Avoid multiple cleanings by submerging the brushes' bristles in paint thinner between coats.

FINISHING TIP

Varnishing Hang Up

I always felt the need for a second pair of hands when it came to varnishing shelves or doors.

A good solution is to hang them up. A series of eyehooks screwed into the floor joists turned my shop ceiling into a helping hand. Two hooks screwed into both ends of each shelf allow them to be suspended in mid-air where I can varnish all the sides with ease. A length of bailing wire with loops twisted on the ends is hooked on the bottom pair of hooks to steady the shelf while finishing.

David Banister
Tallahassee, FL

Saturate the raw surface with distilled water to eliminate a possible catastrophe. Moisture (from rain or wet fingerprints, for example) that inadvertently gets on the surface leaves invisible marks that show up as ugly splotches when stain is applied.

Remove factory sanding marks by carefully and thoroughly sanding with the grain by hand, using 120 grit paper. These factory sanding marks are especially problematic on the rails, where the scratches run across the grain.

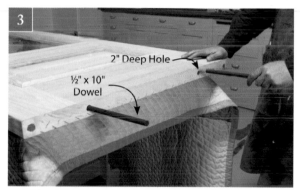

Install hardwood dowels to create temporary legs for standing the door for finishing. Fill the holes with epoxy putty after the finishing process has been completed.

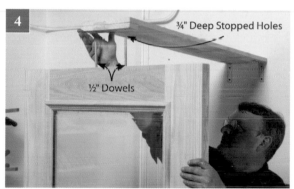

Stabilize the standing door with additional dowels and a wall-mounted bracket, so both faces and all the edges can be finished at once. Coating every surface is important for protection and is required by the manufacturers' warranties.

Apply stain, starting at the bottom, including the bottom edge. Work up one side and adjacent edge, across the top and down the other side and edge. Then move to the other side and repeat the process.

Marine spar varnish developed and tested for use on boats provides the best looking, longest lasting clear exterior finish. You'll pay a premium price to buy it, but it's worth every penny.

Load the brush with varnish and dab off any excess on a clean lint-free cloth to help avoid drips and runs. I prefer a 2" brush with natural china bristles.

Brush the panels first, working from the bottom of the door to the top. This door has only one panel, at the bottom. Start by dabbing finish into the corners and brushing the field that surrounds the raised panel. Then brush the raised panel.

Move on to the rails. Again, start at the bottom of the door (including the bottom edge) and work to the top (including the top edge). Brush the varnish a couple inches beyond the joints with the stiles.

Brush the stiles and edges from bottom to top. Be careful not to brush onto the rails; stop at the joint lines. Check for drips and then move to the other side of the door and repeat the brushing process.

A round sash brush closely follows the molding's shapes and makes it easier to neatly seal the glass to the wood, as recommended by door manufacturers.

Check for drips using a light held at a low angle and remove them by stippling with a small, dry sash brush. Most drips result from varnish scraping off the brush on moldings or raised panels, or from puddling in panel corners.

Use Hidden Areas to Test Finishes

Here's one of the best (and most ignored) tips for getting a great finish: test the stain colors and topcoats you're considering for your masterpiece on its hidden areas. If your piece has no unseen surfaces, use offcuts from the project or leftover scraps of the same wood.

Prepare the areas for your hidden tests as diligently as the parts that show. Record your finishing procedures for each sample. Be sure to topcoat stains and dyes—they usually look totally different under a finish. Aerosol cans of shellac or lacquer work great for this. Be sure to look at your samples under the kind of light the piece will live in—finishes look different under natural or incandescent light than they do under fluorescent shop lights.

Tim Johnson

Offcuts

Inside of
Bed Rail

ART DIRECTION: VERN JOHNSON • PHOTOGRAPHY: MIKE HABERMANN AND BILL ZUEHLKE

by BOB FLEXNER

12 Finishing Tips

GOOD FINISHERS HAVE LOTS OF TRICKS UP THEIR SLEEVES

Add Depth by Glazing

Glazing accentuates the three-dimensional look of moldings, carvings, turnings, and raised panels. A glaze is simply a thickened pigmented stain—thickening it reduces runs on vertical surfaces. Gel stain works well as a glazing material.

Glazing is always done over a sealed surface, meaning over at least one coat of finish. After the first (or second) coat of finish has thoroughly dried, wipe or brush on the glaze. Allow the solvent to evaporate so the glaze dulls. Then wipe off most of the glaze using a rag or brush, leaving some of the glaze in the recessed areas of your project.

After the glaze has dried, apply at least one additional coat of finish. This prevents the glaze from being rubbed or scratched off. Never leave glaze thick; the finish won't bond well to it.

EDITOR: TOM CASPAR • ART DIRECTION: DAVID SIMPSON • PHOTOGRAPHY: BILL ZUEHLKE, UNLESS NOTED

Clean Brushes with Lacquer Thinner

The standard procedure for cleaning a varnish brush is to rinse it a couple of times in mineral spirits, and then wash repeatedly in soap and water. I take an extra step: After the mineral spirits, I rinse my brush in lacquer thinner. Commercial brush cleaner works well, too.

Lacquer thinner or brush cleaner quickly removes most of the oily mineral spirits. This step makes washing with soap and water easier and quicker. You'll usually need only one or two soap-and-water washings to achieve a good lather, which indicates the bristles are clean.

Remember to use adequate ventilation when you work with lacquer thinner or brush cleaner.

Keep Everything Clean

Reduce dust nibs by keeping your project and work area clean. If you are finishing in the same area where you've been sanding, allow time for the dust to settle and then vacuum the floor. Vacuum your project using the brush attachment. Use a lint-free cloth to remove any dust that remains in the wood's pores.

Just before you begin brushing or spraying, wipe your hand over horizontal surfaces to be sure they are clean. You will feel dust you don't see. Your hand will also pick up small bits of dust that may have settled after you did the major cleaning.

Bury Raised Grain

Water-based stain and finish raise wood fibers, making the wood's surface feel rough. Many folks suggest prewetting bare wood with water and sanding the raised grain after the wood dries. This method is fairly effective, but there's an easier way.

Skip the prewetting and bury the raised grain in the finish. Burying simply means encasing the raised grain in a layer of finish. Apply the first coat of water-based finish and then sand it smooth, raised grain and all.

You can use the same approach with a water-based stain, which also raises the grain. The stained surface may become rough, but don't sand the stain. Apply one coat of finish and then sand. Be careful not to cut through the finish into the stain.

Ebonize with Black Dye

The easiest way to make any wood resemble ebony is with black dye. Unlike pigment, which is the colorant used in paint, dye has transparent properties. You can make wood as black as you want and still see the figure of the wood through the dye. I prefer to use walnut when ebonizing because its grain is similar to that of real ebony.

Dyes come in many forms. I prefer to use powdered water-soluble dyes because they offer more time to wipe off the excess. If the wood doesn't become black enough with one coat, make a more intense color or apply one or more extra coats. Allow the dye to dry between coats.

Reveal Flaws in Reflected Light

Something is bound to go wrong when you brush or spray. You may get runs, drips, spills, skips, orange peel—you know the list. The trick is to spot these problems in time to correct them. Reflected light is the answer.

As you finish, move your head so you can see the surface in a reflection of an overhead light, a window, a handheld light or a light on a stand. The reflection's shiny surface will show you the exact condition of the finish.

Wet
Surface

Glue

Find Dried Glue

Dried glue causes spotting when you apply a stain or finish. Most glue dries clear, though, so how can you tell where it is? Water or mineral spirits reveal all.

Before a final sanding, wet the entire surface with water or, if you have adequate ventilation, with mineral spirits. This will make the wood darker, but glue drips, spills and fingerprints will be easily identifiable because they'll appear as a light color. How does this work? Glue seals the wood's surface. Water or mineral spirits won't penetrate the glue spots, so those spots won't become as dark as the rest of the wood.

Water will soften dried glue, making it easier to remove with a card scraper or a chisel. You can also wash off glue by scrubbing with a rag and hot water. When you've removed the glue, sand with the highest grit of sandpaper you used on the rest of the project.

Let Wood Conditioner Dry Thoroughly

Wood conditioners eliminate blotching much better when they're allowed to dry thoroughly. I believe the drying times recommended by manufacturers should be lengthened.

The directions for most solvent-based wood conditioners instruct you to stain within 2 hours of application. These conditioners are actually a varnish, which takes at least 6 to 8 hours to dry in a warm room. It's better to wait overnight before you apply stain.

Most cans of water-based wood conditioners say you can stain 30 minutes after applying the conditioner. I think you should wait at least 2 hours.

Remove Water-Soluble Dye

It happens to everybody. On your sample, the color was perfect, but on your piece, it doesn't look right. Don't despair. There's an easy way to remove water-soluble dye color so you can try again. Sponge the surface liberally with regular household chlorine bleach. Almost instantly the color will lighten and begin to disappear. Two coats of bleach may be necessary and the process may slightly change the color of the raw wood. Rinse everything with water, sand the raised grain, and you've got a second chance.

Synthetic Sponge

ART DIRECTION: JOEL SPIES AND DAVID FARR • PHOTOGRAPHY: KRIVIT PHOTOGRAPHY
CONSULTANT: MICHAEL DRESDNER

Thin the Finish for Better Leveling

Thinning a finish reduces brush marks and orange peel, which are two common problems when you're brushing or spraying. If the finish is thin enough, you can entirely eliminate these defects.

Use the appropriate thinner to thin the finish. Begin by thinning about 10 percent. Thin more, if needed, to achieve better leveling. For water-based finishes, it's best to use the manufacturer's "flow additive" to thin the finish. Adding a little water may help somewhat, but if you add too much, the finish will bead on the surface.

All finishes can be thinned. Sometimes instructions say not to thin a finish, but this is done to comply with EPA volatile organic compound (VOC) laws so less solvent evaporates into the atmosphere. No harm is done to the finish if it is thinned. Thinning does make a finish more likely to run on a vertical surface and to build at a slower rate, however. You may have to apply more coats than usual.

Reduce Blotching in Pine

Staining pine can be a risky business. Some stains cause pine to look blotchy with irregular light and dark areas. Wood conditioners are widely used to reduce blotching prior to staining. For pine, though, using gel stain is far easier, more effective and more predictable than applying wood conditioner for achieving the intensity of color you desire.

In my experience, gel stain is not as effective at reducing blotching on hardwoods, such as cherry, birch, maple or poplar. For these woods, use a wood conditioner before staining.

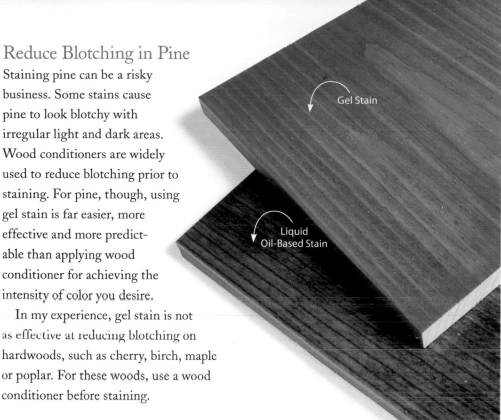

Gel Stain

Liquid Oil-Based Stain

Sand More on End Grain

End grain can turn very dark when stained. More often than not, the problem is that the end grain is still somewhat rough from sawing. The same sanding procedure that you used on the rest of your project is often inadequate to prepare end grain for staining.

To remove saw marks, begin sanding end grain with a coarser paper than you are using on the side grain. An 80-grit sandpaper is usually coarse enough. When you have made the end grain smooth with this grit, work up through the grits just as you do with side grain, finishing with the same grit you used to finish-sand the side grain.

You can make sanding any end grain easier by sealing it with thinned glue or finish before you begin sanding. Thin a white or yellow glue with about three parts water. Thin any finish by about half with the appropriate solvent. Both methods stiffen the fibers, making them easier to cut off with the sandpaper.

Best Finish
For Every Wood

Choosing the best finish for any wood requires finding a match between the color and characteristics of the wood itself, and the service requirements for durability and environmental resistance. It's also important that it be the right color and that it look right. At the end of the job, you can add depth and richness to most pieces of furniture by adding a glaze to emphasize light and shadow. The principles and techniques shared here will help you create the finish that's best for the job.

To make new cherry wood look dark and old without making it blotchy, seal the pores of the wood first, then wipe on a gel stain, page 100.

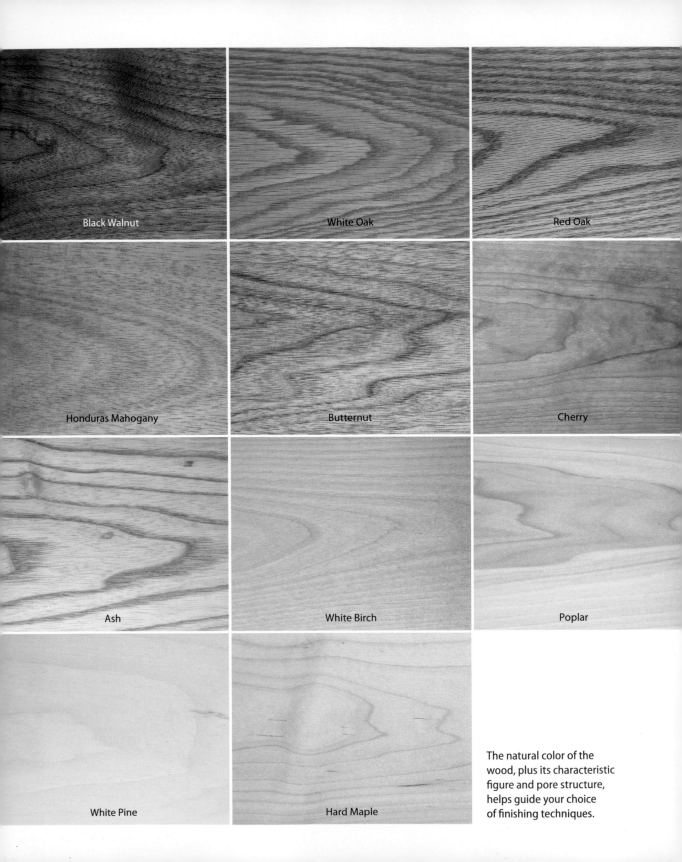

Black Walnut

White Oak

Red Oak

Honduras Mahogany

Butternut

Cherry

Ash

White Birch

Poplar

White Pine

Hard Maple

The natural color of the wood, plus its characteristic figure and pore structure, helps guide your choice of finishing techniques.

by KEVIN SOUTHWICK

Guide to Finishing 11 Common Woods

IMPROVE YOUR RESULTS BY UNDERSTANDING WOOD CHARACTERISTICS

Each species of wood has unique finishing characteristics, both positive and negative. To help you determine how to choose the right wood and get the best results when you finish your next project, I'll explain those characteristics and sum them up in a chart that divides 11 commonly used woods into categories that affect their finished appearance. The notations in each category are based on my observations and experiences with these woods as a professional wood finisher over the past 15 years.

Large pores in earlywood

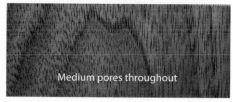

Medium pores throughout

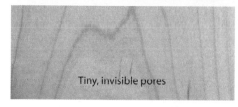

Tiny, invisible pores

Pore Structure

Each species of wood is unique in appearance, thanks mainly to variations between its earlywood and latewood, but also because of the size and distribution of its pores. Pore structure is important when finishing, because most stains accentuate the pores. In ash, pores appear in the earlywood, but not in the latewood, so staining creates a strong contrast between these two elements. In walnut, the pores are evenly distributed across the earlywood and latewood, so staining creates a more uniform appearance. In maple, the pores are so small they're virtually invisible—until stain is applied. Then they appear as dark specks that cover the surface. Also, in oak, walnut and many other species, the pores are large enough to appear as crevices when a clear finish is applied. If a glass-smooth surface is desired, these woods require extra finishing steps to fill the pores.

Fresh Planed Cherry

Aged Cherry

Fresh-Planed Color and Natural Color Change

All types of wood, even finished woods, change color over time, as the result of exposure to air and light. Both the color and the rate of change can vary widely. For example, cherry and maple darken relatively quickly; walnut and mahogany slowly become lighter. Knowing what color the wood will eventually become is important for finishing. It may affect whether or not you decide to use stain, for example. And if you want the Morris chair you're building to look authentic, it's important to know what colors to add to make that new quartersawn white oak look like it's 100 years old.

Sandability and Minimum Final Grit

When is it time to stop sanding? The answer depends on the type of wood and the type of finish. Basically, it's as soon as you can no longer see any sanding scratches. Dense, hard woods with smooth texture and small pores require the most effort and sanding to the highest grits. Woods with large or medium size pores allow stopping at lower grits, because the coarse texture helps to disguise the scratches. The chart indicates the minimum grit at which you can quit sanding for a clear varnish finish. Sand more carefully if you plan to stain the wood—scratches that won't show with a clear finish are likely show up when you stain.

Many woodworkers sand to finer grits for oil finishes.

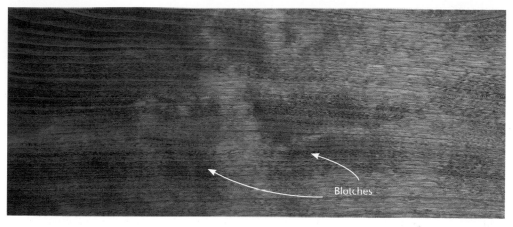
Blotches

Stainability

Many types of wood stain well with oil-based pigment stains. The color soaks in readily and evenly and the results look good. However, some woods are difficult to stain dark, due to their density. And some woods are tricky to stain due to blotching, the random, uneven and unattractive absorption of stain. For woods that are difficult to stain dark, apply multiple coats of pigment stain or start with a dark-colored dye stain. Stain controllers or wood conditioners can be used to minimize blotching.

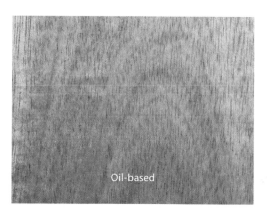
Oil-based

Water-based

The Effect of a Clear Finish

Oil- and water-based finishes have very different effects on a wood's finished color. Oil-based finishes typically add a slight amber tone that benefits dark colored woods such as cherry, but can give maple and other light colored woods an unwanted yellow tone. Water-based finishes add little to no color, keeping light-colored woods looking natural, but leaving dark-colored woods looking pale, or even parched. Orange (amber) shellac resembles an oil-based finish. Blonde (clear) shellac and nitrocellulose lacquer add less color than oil-based finishes, but more than water-based finishes.

Finishing Characteristics of Common Woods (a)

Species	Pore Structure	Fresh-Planed Color (b)	Natural Color Change (c)	Sandability and Minimum Final Grit (d)	Stainability	Effect of Clear Finish
Ash	Pore size: Large. Location: Earlywood only; creates very strong grain patterns. Glass-smooth finish: Filling required.	Sapwood: Pale tan to very light golden brown. Heartwood: Darker.	Slightly darker and more yellow-gold.	Difficult. Stop at 120 grit. Coarse grain helps to hide sanding scratches.	Good. Challenging to make dark without using a multiple-step staining process.	Oil-based: Adds a warmer golden tone. Water-based: Color remains light.
Butternut	Pore size: Medium. Location: Throughout. Glass-smooth finish: Filling required.	Heartwood: Light greyish, greenish, or pinkish brown. Sapwood: White.	Lighter, to a uniform golden brown, and the pores lose their dark color.	Easy to Medium. Stop at 150 grit. Coarse grain helps to hide sanding scratches. Can contain fuzzy areas.	Excellent. Stains dark easily with pigment stain or dye stain.	Oil-based: Darkens and enriches color. Water-based: Color remains light.
Cherry	Pore size: Small. Location: Throughout, but more prominent in earlywood. Glass-smooth finish: Filling not required.	Heartwood: Light pinkish to medium reddish brown. Sapwood: White.	Darker reddish brown, although the intensity can vary greatly.	Medium to Difficult. Stop at 180 grit. Higher grits are required to hide sanding scratches.	Mediocre. Prone to blotching. (e) Pores appear as dark specks when stained. (e)	Oil-based: Darkens and enriches the color. Water-based: Color becomes pale and washed out.
Hard Maple	Pore size: Very small. Location: Throughout. Glass-smooth finish: Filling not required.	Sapwood: Very pale tan. Heartwood: Dark brown.	Slightly darker and more golden.	Difficult. Stop at 180 grit. Higher grits are required to hide sanding scratches.	Mediocre. Prone to blotching. (e) Pores appear as dark specks when stained. (e)	Oil-based: Adds a warmer golden tone. Water-based: Color remains light.
Mahogany	Pore size: Medium. Location: Throughout. Glass-smooth finish: Filling required.	Heartwood: Light to medium reddish brown. Sapwood: Light to medium reddish brown.	Usually less reddish, lighter, more golden brown.	Easy to Medium. Stop at 150 grit. The grain helps to hide sanding scratches. The density of different types of mahogany can vary widely.	Excellent. Stains dark easily with pigment stain or dye stain.	Oil-based: Darkens and enriches the color. Water-based: Color becomes pale and washed out.
Poplar	Pore size: Small. Location: Throughout. Glass-smooth finish: Filling not required.	Sapwood: White. Heartwood: Green; sometimes includes dark purple or black streaks.	Sapwood: Golden brown. Heartwood: Dark brown.	Easy. Stop 150 grit. Low density makes sanding go faster.	Mediocre. Prone to blotching. (e)	Oil-based: Adds a warmer golden tone to sapwood and darkens the heartwood. Water-based: Sapwood remains light; heartwood looks washed out.

Species	Pore Structure	Fresh-Planed Color (b)	Natural Color Change (c)	Sandability and Minimum Final Grit (d)	Stainability	Effect of Clear Finish
Red Oak	Pore size: Very large. Location: Earlywood only; creates very strong grain patterns. Glass-smooth finish: Filling required.	Heartwood: Tan to slightly pinkish brown. Sapwood: White.	Slightly darker and more golden.	Medium. Stop at 120 grit. Coarse grain helps to hide sanding scratches.	Good. Challenging to make dark without using a multiple-step staining process.	Oil-based: Adds a warmer golden tone. Water-based: color remains light.
Black Walnut	Pore size: Medium. Location: Throughout. Glass-smooth finish: Filling required.	Heartwood: Dark greyish brown with purple highlights. (f) Sapwood: Greyish brown to white.	Lighter and more golden brown.	Medium. Stop at 150 grit. Coarse grain helps to hide sanding scratches.	Excellent. Stains dark easily with pigment stain or dye stain.	Oil-based: Darkens and enriches the color. Water-based: Color becomes pale and washed out.
White Birch	Pore size: Small. Location: Throughout. Glass-smooth finish: Filling not required.	Sapwood: Pale, slightly golden brown. Heartwood: Dark brown.	Slightly darker and more golden.	Medium. Stop at 150 grit.	Mediocre. Prone to blotching. (e) Pores appear as dark specks when stained. (e)	Oil-based: Adds a warmer golden tone. Water-based: Color remains light.
White Oak	Pore size: Large. Location: Earlywood only; creates very strong grain patterns. Glass-smooth finish: Filling required.	Sapwood: Tan to very light greyish brown. Heartwood: Darker.	Slightly darker and more golden.	Very Difficult. Stop at 120 grit. Coarse grain helps to hide sanding scratches.	Good. Challenging to make dark without using a multiple-step staining process.	Oil-based: Adds a warmer golden tone. Water-based: Color becomes pale and washed-out.
White Pine	Pore size: None—coniferous. Location: NA Glass-smooth finish: Filling not required.	Heartwood: Pale tan. Sapwood: Pale tan.	Slightly darker and more golden brown.	Easy. Stop at 150 grit. Low density makes sanding go faster.	Mediocre. Prone to blotching. (c) Earlywood is much more absorbent to stain and finish than latewood.	Oil-based: Adds a warmer golden tone. Water-based: Color remains light.

Notes:

a) The appearance of virtually any species of wood can vary widely, so exceptions to the notations will surely occur.

b) The preferred choice for color (heartwood or sapwood) is listed first.

c) Long-term exposure to direct sunlight causes many woods to fade.

d) Minimum final sanding grit for a clear varnish finish.

e) Wood conditioner minimizes blotching and specking, but makes the wood difficult to stain dark without using a multiple-step staining process.

f) Describes kiln-dried walnut. Air-dried walnut heartwood is medium brown with red and gold highlights.

by KEVIN SOUTHWICK

Match Any Finish

STEP BOARDS SHOW THE WAY TO PERFECT MISSION OAK

Wiping paint thinner on a board gives a pretty good idea of the color you can expect from a clear, low sheen oil-based finish. And often, a few quick stain samples will be good enough to choose an acceptable color. But there are also times when "pretty good" and "good enough" won't do. Suppose you've built a blanket chest to complete the antique bedroom set your spouse inherited from dear Aunt Irene. If you don't replicate the set's 100-year-old patina, the chest will never truly match the other pieces. Step-by-step sample boards (called "step boards") are the solution, because they allow you to build the finish layer by layer, just like the patina of that antique finish.

Step Boards Are Essential

Why take chances when it comes to finishing any project? Simply put, making step boards is the best way to ensure success, because they allow you to dial in the perfect finish on replaceable wood, rather than on your project. In addition, experimenting on step boards gives you the freedom to make mistakes and learn important lessons about different finishing materials and methods.

Step boards are very different from stain samples at a store, or samples made by hastily wiping stain on an offcut. Step boards are carefully planned to show every step in a finishing process, so you can clearly see the effect of each step. Step boards can do much more than eliminate bad color choices. They can provide surprising answers to simple questions (see "Step Board Q&A," page 91). Step boards can expose unexpected problems such as blotching, or allow you to learn the best way to highlight the wood's figure. Whenever you're working with a new type of wood, a new finishing product, or a new application method, it's a good idea to make step boards.

Good Investments

The time, money and effort you spend to create step boards are good investments. A collection of completed step boards is a valuable tool for comparing finishes or for plotting a course for a new finish.

These step boards helped create the perfect match for a traditional Mission Oak finish. The final recipe's on page 91.

Such a collection increases in value over time, because you gain experience and information with each new addition. As a professional finisher, I use step boards to ensure that my clients' expectations are crystal clear and to ensure consistency throughout big projects. In a nutshell, properly prepared step boards turn finishing from a guessing game into a problem-solving process that guarantees predictable results.

No Short Cuts

Making accurate step boards requires the same methodical approach and attention to detail that's required to complete any complex woodworking task. Follow these instructions to control variables and ensure reliable results.

- Carefully select the wood to represent the appropriate quality, cut, grain and figure of the wood used in your project. Each board must be large enough (6" x 20" to 30") to clearly show every step, including a large sample (at least 6" x 8") of the completed finish.
- Buy enough lumber. If your project includes plywood, molding or carving with exposed end grain, include samples of each.
- Prepare the surface exactly the same as on the project. Use the same sanding materials and processes.
- Apply all stain products in the same manner as on the project and with the same timing.
- Apply topcoats using the same methods and materials. Different topcoats can have a significant effect on color and sheen. Allow proper dry time and include sanding between coats, when appropriate.

- Record the materials and application methods you use for each and every step. Mark the step board itself or keep a finishing notebook.

Match a Finish

Making step boards is the best way to discover how valuable they can be. The process will open your eyes to the way various finishing materials work separately and in different combinations. Once you've made step boards for several different projects, you'll be amazed how adept you've become at knowing how to create interesting finishes that enhance the pieces for which they're designed.

To get you started, I'll use step boards to solve a difficult challenge—matching an authentic "mission oak" finish. I'll demonstrate the process and give you the recipe. Your job is to locate a worthy piece of quartersawn white oak and make your own step board to catalog this attractive finish.

Successfully matching an existing finish requires diagnostic skills that come with finishing experience, because the process involves layering different colors and finishes. The best way to develop these skills is to experiment on step boards and observe the results. Use the information each board provides to guide your next effort.

The finish I'm going to match appears on an old drawer front made of quartersawn white oak. It has golden, glowing rays, a dark brown hue, black pores, an amber tone and a low sheen.

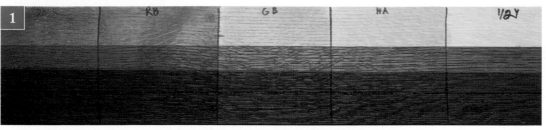

Dye Stains

Pigment Stain

Amber Shellac

Step boards show the effect that each individual component has on the overall appearance of a finish. This board shows three different components layered on top of each other. Specifically, it tests how different dye stain ground colors affect the final appearance.

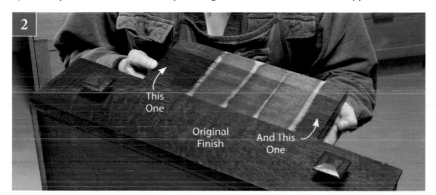

This One

Original Finish

And This One

Step boards are essential tools for matching a finish, such as the original finish on this old Mission style drawer. This step board tests several pigment stains layered between yellow dye and amber shellac, two other components that the new finish is sure to include. Two of the stains look promising and warrant a closer look on separate step boards.

Experience tells me that the best way to imitate the intensely colored rays is to use a golden brown or yellow dye as a ground color. I know that I can replicate the dark brown tone and black pores with an oil-based pigment stain. I can duplicate the amber tone by using orange/amber shellac (which I'm sure is the original finish), and I can achieve the low sheen by applying a topcoat of satin varnish. Now that I've identified the basic components of the finish, I can start making step boards. As the overall color of the finish is created by layering dye stain, pigment stain and shellac, I'll use all three components to determine the exact color of each one. On my first step board, the dye color is the variable; the pigment stain and the shellac are consistent (Photo 1). On my second step board, the pigment stain is the variable (Photo 2).

The next step is to make a pair of complete step boards, so that I can compare the two promising finishes that I've identified. Each board must be large enough to adequately show each finish layer, with a large section at the end showing the completed finish. These large samples make it easier to choose the one that matches the best. One interesting thing about step boards is that the finish doesn't look right until the last layer is applied (Photo 3). For each finish layer you add on the step board, follow the same application method and drying time that you'll use on your project (Photo 4).

Using amber shellac to match the amber tone of the original finish may take some experimenting. With one coat of shellac, the amber tone of my step boards looked pale,

Make a large step board for each of the two promising stains, so you can compare them both to the original finish. After taping off the first 3" to retain the board's natural color, apply the yellow dye ground color to the rest of each board.

Tape off the next 3" on each board. Then apply one (or the other) pigment stain and wipe it off. Taping off isolates each finish step, so it will show as a band on each completed board.

Second Coat

First Coat of Shellac

Reposition the tape on each board and apply two coats of amber shellac. Allow the first coat to dry. Then move the tape and apply the second coat.

Move the tape on each board for the final time and apply the water-based polyurethane topcoat.

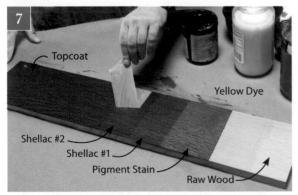

Topcoat

Yellow Dye

Shellac #2

Shellac #1

Pigment Stain

Raw Wood

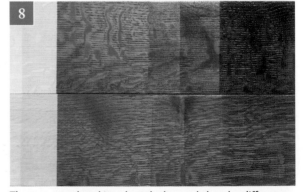

Each completed step board clearly shows the progression from raw wood to completed finish.

The two completed step boards show subtle color differences due to a single variable—slightly different dark brown pigment stains. The bottom step board matches the drawer's original finish very nicely—we have a winner!

compared to the drawer's original finish. So, I applied a second coat (Photo 5).

Applying the topcoat is the last step (Photo 6). Each completed board clearly shows every finishing step (Photo 7). I now have two similar—but distinct—finishes to choose from (Photo 8). And as I've recorded every step, I can easily duplicate them both.

The "Mission Oak" Recipe

Materials

- TransFast yellow water-soluble dye (powder form), mixed at half the label strength.
- Bartley's jet mahogany gel stain.
- Zinsser amber shellac, 2 lb cut.
- General Finishes water-based high-performance polyurethane, satin.

How-to

1. Finish sand all surfaces to 150 grit.
2. Apply the dye liberally, let it saturate the wood for a couple minutes, and then wipe off the excess. Allow the dye to completely dry—usually about one hour.
3. Apply the gel stain liberally and immediately wipe off the excess. The working time for gel stains is about five minutes, so work in relatively small areas. Allow the stain to dry twelve hours.
4. Brush on two coats of shellac, allowing ½ hour dry time following each coat.
5. Scuff the shellac with a gray nylon abrasive pad.
6. Brush on one or more water-based polyurethane topcoats.

Step Board Q & A

Step boards can provide definitive answers to finishing questions, because they allow testing each variable independently. The results can be subtle, or surprising. For example:

"How does a clear finish change the color of the wood?"
A clear finish can produce a variety of colors, depending on the number of coats that are applied. The color of this walnut board deepens dramatically as the wood becomes fully saturated and a film builds on top.

"What does the yellow dye do?"
When used as a ground color on the raw wood, yellow water-based dye helps to create the nuances found in mission-era finishes on quartersawn white oak. Most importantly, it colors the rays and intensifies their appearance. It also enriches the color of the dark brown stain and blackens the pores.

"Why use amber shellac?"
Wow! As you can see, amber shellac literally transforms the color when it's applied over layers of dye and pigment. Its unique effect is a key element in creating authentic-looking finishes for Arts and Crafts-style furniture pieces.

by RICHARD HELGESON

Coloring Figured Wood

TWO DYES AND A GLAZE CREATE A STUNNING EFFECT

Apply a coat of black dye. Let the panel dry.

Figured wood is a finisher's delight. Just put a good topcoat on curly maple and you'll begin to see the three-dimensional effect. When you color the wood with dyes and emphasize its figure with a glaze, wow! The curly maple becomes ripples on a pond, a perfect illusion and a beautiful accent.

Start with Black

First, mix up a batch of black aniline dye. Apply the dye using a foam brush (Photo 1). Let the dye soak in and dry at least 1 hour. Next, sand off most of the dye with 180 grit paper (Photo 2). I use an orbital sander for the bulk of the work, then go back and sand areas that look too mottled, using a cork or felt block.

Black dye adds extra depth to the wood's figure. Sanding removes the dye from areas where the dye didn't penetrate very deep, and leaves the dye in areas that are more absorbent. The result is a pattern of dark areas that look like shadows, and this makes the curly grain appear more three-dimensional. Sanding also removes any wood fibers raised by the water in the dye.

Sand off most of the dye. Areas where the dye remains will look like shadows.

Figured maple colored with dyes and enhanced with a glaze can look like ripples on a pond.

Add Bright Colors

Next, mix up a brightly colored dye and brush it on the panel (Photo 3). Let the panel dry overnight, then apply two to three coats of 2 lb. cut dewaxed shellac. I use Bulls Eye SealCoat, which is premixed as a 2 lb. cut. Topcoats will adhere better to dewaxed shellac than to standard shellac. I use a simple folded pad to apply the shellac (Photo 4), but a brush would work just as well.

Your panel should be looking pretty good at this point, but an additional step of adding a glaze will make it look much better (Photo 5). I often use a glaze that's basically the same color as the dye, but darker. If you're adventurous, try experimenting with different colors. Adding this layer makes the finish look much richer and more complex.

A glaze is simply a pigmented finish that's applied over a sealed surface. (The surface is sealed—with shellac, in this case—to prevent the glaze from penetrating too deeply and unevenly.) You can buy ready-made glazes at an art-supply store, but I prefer a wider choice of colors, so I make my own. The recipe is very simple. I use a tube of artist's oil color for the pigment, mineral spirits to thin the pigment, and a clear gel varnish to bind the pigment to the surface. The exact ratios aren't critical. For this small panel, I squirted out about 1" of pigment from the tube and mixed it with about ½ capful of mineral spirits, stirring until there were no lumps. Next, I mixed about 1 teaspoon of mineral spirits with 2 teaspoons of gel varnish, and added the thinned pigment.

Apply a brightly colored dye, such as blue or green.

Wipe on three coats of super-blonde dewaxed shellac.

Add depth to the finish by wiping on a thin coat of brightly-colored glaze.

Apply gel varnish or any other topcoat.

Wipe on the glaze with a piece of cheesecloth, using a circular motion. Then lightly wipe the panel with the cheesecloth, using a straight motion, to even out the glaze. You can remove or leave as much glaze as you wish, or apply a second coat later on. Let the panel dry overnight, then apply more coats of plain gel varnish, or any other finish (Photo 6).

FINISHING TIP

Applying Bright-Colored Stains

Ground pigment stains can now offer you bright, transparent colors that are clear and colorfast—a combination of the best features of stains and dyes. They're highly concentrated—as the tiny bottles attest.

Here's a trick for evenly applying these concentrated colors to a large surface: First, wet the wood with mineral spirits. This makes it easy to add and spread the color which won't soak in right away because the surface is saturated. Instead the color mixes with the solvent and slowly soaks in as you spread it around. To deepen the color, work in more of the concentrate.

*Tim Johnson &
Dave Munkittrick*

Mineral Spirits

ART DIRECTION: JOEL SPIES AND DAVID FARR • PHOTOGRAPHY: KRIVIT PHOTOGRAPHY
CONSULTANT: MICHAEL DRESDNER

by KEVIN SOUTHWICK

Make Poplar Look Pretty

GIVE THIS USEFUL BUT UNATTRACTIVE WOOD A MAKEOVER

The wood we know as poplar has many common names, such as tulip poplar, yellow poplar, tulipwood, yellow tulipwood, tulip tree, whitewood and canoewood. The "tulip" part of these names comes from the tulip-like flower the tree produces in the spring. Where the "poplar" part of these names comes from is a mystery, because the tree is not even a true poplar—it's a member of the magnolia family. In fact, poplar is known as the "king of the Magnolias." It's also the tallest hardwood tree in North America.

Regardless of what it's called, *Liriodendron tulipifera Magnoliaceae* produces very useful and versatile lumber. The tree grows fast, with a straight trunk and no branches near the ground. That translates to knot-free boards that are available in expansive widths and thicknesses. Poplar is economical, costing considerably less than other hardwoods such as maple and oak, and its finely textured lumber works well with both hand and power tools. These qualities make poplar suitable for many furniture and construction applications.

See how to transform this plain poplar table in eight easy steps.

Start by wiping on a strong stain controller to keep the poplar from blotching when you apply the dye and stain. Make a strong stain controller by thinning gel varnish with mineral spirits.

An Ugly Duckling

So why isn't poplar popular with furniture makers? The answer is simple: The wood is just plain homely. Its color ranges from pale yellowish white to an odd shade of green, and boards are often discolored by dark gray or purplish streaks. To top it off, poplar doesn't stain well with traditional wood stains. In fact, it can get ugly really fast because it blotches so easily. About the only time furniture makers use poplar as a primary wood is when the piece is going to be painted.

Transformed

Poplar has too many desirable furniture-making qualities to be limited to "paint-grade" service. Fortunately, by using a special approach, it's possible to make this ugly duckling glow beautifully. This process will transform poplar's odd green color to any brown wood tone you like. However, dark streaks will still show—they'll need to be avoided or placed strategically in the design and called "character."

The key to giving poplar a rich, even stain color is to control its horrible blotching tendencies. This requires starting with a very effective stain controller (also called wood conditioner or pre-stain sealer). The commercial stain controllers I tested didn't provide enough blotch resistance, so I developed a simple recipe to make a controller with the necessary strength. This recipe and the finishing steps that follow work well on any wood that's prone to blotching.

After applying the stain controller, use a two-step coloring process for better control and color intensity. This coloring method combines the benefits of both dye and pigment stain. The dye provides a ground color as strong and rich as needed, and the pigment ensures that the color doesn't fade and become dull over time. The dye and pigment colors shown here are both a medium-dark "warm" brown. They combine to create a rich chocolaty tone on both the green heartwood and pale sapwood. Your color choices may be different.

How-to

1. Prepare the surfaces by sanding to 180 grit. Be sure to sand by hand after you power sand, to eliminate swirl marks. Pay extra attention to the end grain.
2. To make the stain controller, mix one part General Finishes Clear Gel Varnish with three parts paint thinner. Apply the stain controller with a rag and allow it to soak in (Photo 1). Be sure to saturate the wood, especially the end grain. After a couple of minutes, but before the stain controller starts to set up (5-10

Wash the sealed surface with soap and water so the dye will soak in, rather than bead up on the surface.

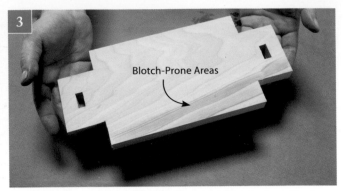

Blotch-Prone Areas

Blotch-prone areas will stand out as the water dries, because they're super-absorbent. After the wood has thoroughly dried, apply an additional coat of stain controller to these areas.

minutes), use clean, dry rags to remove any that has not soaked in. Be sure not to leave any wet spots or streaks—they'll show up when you apply the stain. Let the wood dry overnight. This step is intended to seal the wood approximately 60%-75%, which is usually enough to control blotching and still allow the stain to penetrate.

3. Wash the partially sealed surface with a mixture of dish soap and water to "open" the top layer of wood cells so they'll absorb the dye easily (Photo 2). This step won't cause any significant grain-raising because the surface has been treated with the stain controller.

4. Hidden blotches will reveal themselves as the water dries (Photo 3). Areas that are extra-porous soak up more water. This means they'll stay wet longer, so they're easy to identify. The longer they stay wet, the worse the blotch will be. Fortunately, even super-absorbent areas can be tamed if they're found and treated with extra stain controller before color is applied.

5. Mix TransFast Medium Brown Water Based Dye following the label instructions and apply it generously, using a rag (Photo 4). Allow the dye to saturate the wood, then remove the excess with clean rags. Allow the wood to dry until the water has completely evaporated (2 hours).

6. Check the workpiece and selectively apply clear gel to any blotches or end grain that are already dark enough from the dye step (Photo 5). This is your last chance for blotch reducing.

7. Apply a coat of General Finishes Medium Brown Gel Stain (Photo 6). Then let the piece dry overnight.

8. Apply two coats of 2 lb. cut amber shellac (Photo 7). Although shellac is a durable finish, I know that this table will often be used as a place to rest a coffee cup, so I'll add a coat of oil-based satin polyurethane to prevent water rings.

Apply a coat of medium-brown dye to create a uniform ground color.

Look again for blotching or dark end grain. Seal any areas that have gone extra-dark with a coat of gel varnish just before you apply the gel stain in the next step.

Apply a coat of medium-brown gel stain. Gel stain adds richness to the overall color and helps to keep the dye from fading.

Apply two coats of amber shellac to add depth and tone, followed by a more protective topcoat, if necessary.

Turn Green to Gold

Oxalic acid works miracles on poplar's green heartwood. Simply mix a saturated solution of oxalic crystals in hot water and brush the solution on the wood. As the solution dries, the green heartwood will turn to a golden brown and the white sapwood will take on a warmer shade of pale. A second application of the solution after the first has thoroughly dried usually helps the results—and it can't hurt. Oxalic acid is poisonous, so let the surface dry completely and then rinse it thoroughly with water to remove any acid that remains. Note that this treatment does nothing to reduce poplar's tendency to blotch, so you'll still need to follow the recipe to end up with a great-looking finish.

Oxalic acid is primarily used to restore the natural color of grayed, weathered, exterior wood—it's the active ingredient in deck-renewing products. Restorers and woodworkers use oxalic acid to remove black water stains from wood. It's available at most hardware stores.

by TIM JOHNSON

Aged Cherry Finish

WIPE ON YEARS OF AGE IN A FEW EASY STEPS

If you want to make a woodworker gnash his teeth, ask him to make new cherry look like cherry that has aged naturally to a rich, brownish hue.

Why is this challenge so fiendish? Because staining cherry, even with stain that's the perfect color, doesn't do the trick.

Here's why: Cherry's surface is covered with legions of tiny pores that are almost impossible to see—until you apply stain. Stain turns these pores dark, so they stand out. Naturally aged cherry doesn't show dark pores; so it's impossible to create an authentic look with stain alone.

Production shops solve the problem by spraying on toned lacquer finishes; old masters pad on shellac and hand-mixed glaze. Here's a no-fuss method that uses off-the-shelf products and produces great results.

1. Wipe on a coat of General Finishes' Gel Topcoat clear urethane finish (Photo 1, at right). Apply the finish generously, using an overlapping a circular motion to work the finish into the pores. Remove the excess finish by wiping across the grain, followed by wiping with the grain. After the finish is thoroughly dry (6 to 8 hours in good conditions), lightly scuff the surface with 320 grit sandpaper or 0000 steel wool.

2. Wipe on a second coat of Gel Topcoat. Let it dry and lightly scuff the surface as before.

3. Wipe on a coat of General Finishes' Candlelite gel stain (Photo 2). I think it's the perfect color for aging cherry. As this stain sets up pretty quickly, divide the work into manageable sections. Apply the stain liberally, then wipe with the grain to remove the excess. The trick is to remove all the streaks, blotches and rag marks while leaving as much color on the surface as you can. A rag that's partially loaded with stain works best. I like to use two rags: one more heavily loaded than the other, so that I can add color and remove marks as needed. When you're done, take a

Wipe on two coats of General Finishes' Gel Topcoat, after finish-sanding to 180 grit. Let each coat dry thoroughly. This step seals the wood's pores.

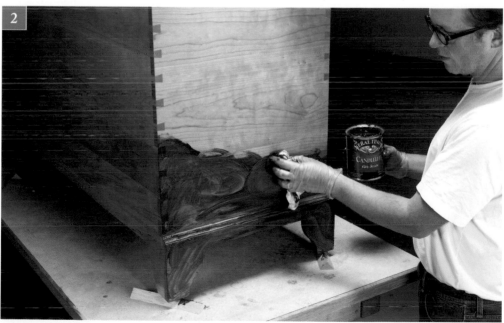

Wipe on one or more coats of General Finishes' Candlelite gel stain. Because the wood's surface is sealed, the gel stain adds an even layer of color that makes cherry look like it has aged naturally.

careful look in good light to make sure the color is uniform and goof-free. Let the finish dry thoroughly.

4. Wipe on a second coat of Candlelite gel stain to deepen the tone.

5. Protect the color layer by wiping on additional coats of Gel Topcoat. For wear surfaces, such as table tops, you could opt to build a more durable finish by brushing or spraying on coats of polyurethane.

Usually you can't apply stain over a finish. But the process works with these gel stains because they're actually colored gel varnish. Applying Candlelite gel stain over Gel Topcoat is similar to applying a layer of toned finish, and because the wood's surface has already been sealed, the stain doesn't darken the pores. This method reduces blotching, for the same reason. Another benefit of sealing the wood before staining is that if you don't like the color the stain imparts, you can wipe it off with mineral spirits (as long as the stain is still wet), without harming the Gel Topcoat underneath.

Each additional layer of gel stain deepens the wood's tone. Another way to achieve a deeper tone is to skip Step 2 and apply stain over one coat of clear Topcoat. But as the wood's surface isn't as thoroughly sealed,

you'll end up with some dark pores and a little more blotching. A third method is to simply wait, as the cherry will slowly darken naturally under the stain.

You can alter the wood's tone by using a different gel stain color for the second coat (Step 4). Stains with names such as "brown mahogany," "walnut" or "mission" usually make cherry more brown; "mahogany" and "cherry" stains usually make cherry more red. Always choose gel stain by its color, however, not by its name.

Blend Color Mismatches

Use the same method to blend cherry sapwood and heartwood, plywood and solid wood, and even color variations between boards. Begin by sealing the entire surface with one or two coats of Gel Topcoat. This step also shows the wood's natural color, so you can choose the most complementary stain color: Candlelite gel stain is a great place to start. When the Topcoat has dried, apply Candlelite gel stain to the light-colored sapwood only. Gel stain is perfect for this job, because its thick, no-drip consistency makes it easy to control. When this first coat of stain has dried, apply a second coat of Candlelite gel stain over the entire surface.

Sap Wood

Heart Wood

Gel Topcoat on all.

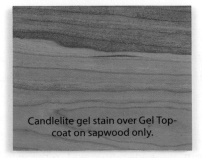

Candlelite gel stain over Gel Topcoat on sapwood only.

Second coat of Candlelite gel stain on all.

1

Dissolve steel wool in vinegar to make the first of two solutions you'll need. The pad should completely dissolve in about one week.

by RICHARD TENDICK

Chemical Ebonizing

A SURE-FIRE RECIPE FOR TURNING ANY WOOD DEEP BLACK

Remember the old ad slogan, "better living through chemistry"? When it comes to turning wood black—a process called ebonizing—I prefer the chemical approach, which uses solutions made from vinegar, steel wool and tannic acid. Watching them transform an ordinary wood, such as the yellow poplar I'm using here, is magical.

Other methods of ebonizing (dye, ink and paint) use pigments, which can obscure the wood's grain. The chemical technique leaves an absolutely transparent layer of black. You can still see the wood's figure and character, particularly after you apply a topcoat.

Woodworkers have long known that rusty, acidic water turns some wood black. Woods that are high in tannic acid, such as oak, walnut and mahogany, work best. The technique I'll show you adds tannic acid to the wood, so you

EDITOR: TOM CASPAR • PHOTOGRAPHY: JASON ZENTNER

can ebonize virtually any species. I can't take credit for this idea, though; it's been a finisher's trick for a long time.

Mixing the Chemicals

The two solutions can be stored and used over and over. The first is more or less liquid rust, which you make with white vinegar and steel wool (Photo 1). For the best results, use Heinz white vinegar and Liberon 4/0 steel wool. This steel wool works well because it doesn't contain oil, but you could also use regular steel wool and wash out its oil with a detergent. Cover the jar with a lid, then puncture the lid with a small hole to let gas escape. Set the jar aside for a week or so.

Eventually, the pad will dissolve and the formerly clear liquid will turn a dark reddish brown, with a black scum on top. Place a coffee filter in a funnel and pour this gunk through the filter into a new container. Repeat the process two or three times, using new filters, to remove all the solids from the solution.

The second solution, tannic acid, is made with dry powdered tannin. It's not expensive, but unfortunately it's not available in a small quantity. Rather than be stuck with a lifetime's supply, I've shared the surplus with a dozen woodworking friends.

To mix the powder, place 1 heaping tablespoon in a disposable container and add a small amount of water (Photo 2). Stir until the powder forms a paste, then add 1 pint

of hot tap water. Transfer the solution to a jar or bottle. It can be used right away.

The next step is to raise the wood's grain with plain water (Photo 3). This is important to do now, before applying either solution, because you won't be able to sand the wood during the ebonizing process. After the wood dries, sand off any fuzz you may feel with 280 or 320 grit paper (Photo 4). I usually repeat this process two or three times.

Application

It's clear sailing from here. First, pour a small amount of the tannic acid solution into a shallow container and brush it on your project (Photo 5). Make sure every bit of the surface is covered. Let the wood dry.

Next, pour a small amount of the steel wool and vinegar solution into a separate container. Using a different brush, apply the solution to the wood (Photo 6). Almost immediately, the wood will turn a bluish black. Don't pour the excess solution back into your original container, as it will be contaminated by the tannic acid. Again, let the wood dry. Finally, apply another coat of tannic acid, using a rag to avoid brush marks (Photo 7). Voila! You'll get a rich, deep black.

Dispose the surplus tannic acid (it will be contaminated, too), and let the wood dry a day or two. You're ready to apply a clear finish.

Make tannic acid for the second solution. Mix dry powdered tannin with a small amount of water to make a paste, then add more water.

Raise the grain before you begin the ebonizing process. Wet the wood's surface with a damp rag or sponge.

Sand with fine paper to remove any fibers sticking up from the wood's surface.

Brush on the tannic acid solution and let it dry.

Apply the vinegar and steel wool solution. The surface will turn a bluish black right away.

Apply more tannic acid with a rag. This turns the wood a deep, transparent black. After it dries, you're ready for a topcoat.

by KEVIN SOUTHWICK

Glazing Techniques From a Pro

USE GEL STAINS TO ADD RICHNESS, DEPTH AND COLOR

Some wood finishes have richness and depth that combine to create a special warm glow. This glow usually comes with age, resulting from natural changes in the wood, due to its exposure to light, and to a patina that develops at the wood's surface, in and on the finish. By imitating the effects of time, glazing can also create this glow. Basic glazing techniques are easy to learn, and they provide a much faster way to enhance a finish than waiting for Father Time.

Glazing techniques use stains differently than the way they're normally used. Instead of staining the raw wood, glazing is done after a finish has been applied, so instead of soaking in, the color sits on top of the sealed, nonporous surface.

Glazing can be done with any coloring material that will adhere well to a sealed surface (see "Glazing Materials," page 110). Glazing materials need to be thick. Several brands of oil-based gel stains work well as glazes. However, regular thin oil stains don't work well, because they don't contain enough binder to stick to the finish, or enough color to be effective.

In general, oil-based glazing materials are usually easier to work with, because they have a longer working time than water-based materials. They're also easier to remove, if something goes wrong.

Projects of all sizes can be glazed. Here, I'll use a mahogany picture frame to demonstrate how to use a couple of basic glazing techniques to add color and character. These techniques can also be used to change a color for matching purposes, to add a subtle warm tone to an otherwise cold finish, and to age reproduction pieces. Many fancy faux finishing techniques also use glazing methods and materials.

Virtually Goof-proof

Because glazing is done on a sealed surface, it's very forgiving. If you don't like the results, oil-based glaze can easily be erased with mineral spirits, as long as you act before the glaze hardens. (Color will be retained only in areas where the surface is left porous.) This means that almost nothing can go wrong, and you can practice all you want.

Unlike stains, you can apply glazes between coats of finish.

EDITOR: TIM JOHNSON

Technique 1

Start by brushing on thin coats of amber shellac to seal the wood and add a warm tone. Let the shellac dry, then sand lightly

Next, cover the surface with glaze. The simplest method is to generously brush on the glaze using a disposable brush.

Finish by using cheesecloth to wipe off the excess glaze. Cheesecloth provides more control than ordinary cotton rags, so you can leave a little color in grooves and crevices.

The best colors for glazing to imitate the effects of age are in the medium brown range, like dirt. Golden or amber colors are best for adding warmth to a pale finish, such as a clear finish on new pine, birch or maple. The goal for this mahogany frame is to deepen the overall color and enhance the molding and carving by leaving a little more color in the grooves and crevices. The gel stain I'm using is a medium dark brown color that's on the cool side. No thinner was added.

Seal the Surface

The first step for both techniques is to seal the wood so that the glaze can't soak in (Photo 1). Here, I'm using amber (also called orange) shellac for sealing, because of its warm glow and fast dry time, but any film building finish will work. Four coats of 1½-lb cut shellac will ensure thorough sealing and provide an attractive finish. (To create a 1½-lb cut, mix 1 part canned amber shellac with 1 part denatured alcohol.) More coats may be required to fully seal end grain or carvings. Let each coat dry for half an hour. Sand lightly between coats with 400 grit sandpaper or 0000 steel wool. Sand after the last coat, too, to prepare the surface for glazing. The scratches from the fine abrasive will help catch the glaze.

Glazing with cheesecloth

Once the wood has been sealed, the first glazing technique is similar to staining raw wood. You apply the glaze (Photo 2) and then wipe it off (Photo 3). But instead of using an ordinary rag for wiping, you use cheesecloth. Like the bristles of a brush, cheesecloth's loosely woven texture gently removes the glaze from the surface, so you can remove as little or as much as you want. You can remove the glaze uniformly, to leave an even coating of color, or wipe across carvings, flutes and fillets to leave glaze in the crevices.

Glazing with brushes

Round natural bristle sash brushes are hard to beat for applying and removing glaze. They're especially well suited for pushing glaze into corners and grooves. They're also excellent for leaving just the right amount of glaze on the surface to create the desired effect. The best strategy is to use one brush to apply and work the glaze, and a second, clean brush for final touch-up. Start by working a small amount of glaze into the first brush on your disposable palette (Photo 4). Then transfer the glaze to the surface (Photo 5). Sash brushes allow you to apply, work and remove glaze all at the same time. You can add or remove color, work selectively or overall, and you can work crevices as easily as high spots.

As you continue to apply and remove glaze while you work the surface, it's important to keep the brush from becoming overloaded (Photo 6). Switch to the clean brush to finish the job (Photo 7).

The glaze begins to harden and becomes difficult to work after about five minutes. It's important to finish working the glaze before this happens. Remember, it's also possible to remove the glaze and start over. Once you've completed the job, allow the glaze to dry

Technique 2

For maximum control, use a natural bristle sash brush to glaze the sealed surface. Put a small amount of glaze on a palette. Dip the brush in the glaze and then remove the excess on a clean part of the palette.

Dab on the glaze and then brush it out. The sash brush allows you to delicately apply and spread the glaze.

As you work the surface, keep the brush from becoming saturated with glaze by cleaning it on an absorbent towel or rag.

overnight. After the first coat is dry (24 hrs above 60° for gel stains), you can repeat the process to add more color and/or highlights.

The final step is usually to apply clear finish to lock the glaze down under a protective layer, or to provide an appropriate sheen. But if the finished object is more decorative than functional, and the sheen is consistent, this step may not be necessary, as is the case with this frame.

Switch to a clean brush for final glaze removal. It's a good idea to take off your glaze-stained gloves for this step, so you don't mess up the work you've done.

Glazing Materials

Gel stains work well for glazing, but making your own glaze offers unlimited options for color and consistency. To make your own glaze, you need concentrated color, such as japan color or artist's oil, and an oil-based glazing medium to use as a "binder," to make sure the color will adhere to the surface, and to provide a smooth, thick consistency.

Clear gel varnish and artist's glazing medium both work well as binders; artist's glazing medium allows a longer working time. Start by putting a small amount of binder in a mixing container, then add small amounts of color and whisk in with a brush until the desired concentration is reached. Paint thinner or mineral spirits can be added in small amounts (from 5% to 20%) to increase working time. Just remember, glaze needs to be fairly thick to work.

by MITCH KOHANEK

Tips for Using Shellac

MAKE FRIENDS WITH THIS BEAUTIFUL, VERSATILE FINISH

Recently I was asked to judge a woodworking show. One of the best pieces was a wonderfully constructed grandfather clock. Unfortunately, a quick brushing of polyurethane ruined the clock's appearance. The clock's creator said he chose polyurethane for protection. But how durable does a coating on a grandfather clock have to be? Why put a finish originally designed for floors on a beautiful clock? What a difference shellac would have made.

Don't get me wrong, polyurethane is a great choice for high wear surfaces like a desk or kitchen tabletop. However, I find people use poly by default simply because it's readily available as well as durable. But is durability all that matters? There are many other considerations that make shellac a great choice for adding beauty and protection to your projects.

Many woodworkers have walked (stormed) away in frustration after trying shellac. It's a unique finish and there are some fundamental ground rules one must follow. The tips in this story cover the basics that will get you going on the right track.

When you need to match a beautiful old finish, shellac is the best option.

Buying Advice

Should you buy waxed or dewaxed shellac? Wax occurs naturally in shellac. If shellac is going to be the only finish, then shellac with wax works fine. The wax decreases drag when padding or brushing shellac. If shellac is used as a sealer or undercoat for other finishes, choose the dewaxed version to avoid adhesion problems, especially with polyurethane. Dewaxed shellac also has greater clarity and is more heat and water resistant. You can dewax your own shellac by letting the wax settle out and pouring off the clear dewaxed portion.

The next decision a shellac buyer makes is color. A good rule of thumb is to use the darker colors on dark woods and light colors on light woods.

Shellac is a natural product made from lac

beetle (*Lacifer Iacca*) excretions. Shellac comes in colors that range from dark reddish brown to a golden amber color depending on the time of harvest and degree of processing. There are five commonly available grades of shellac from least to most refined: seedlac, buttonlac, garnet, orange and super blonde.

Seedlac is simply collected from the trees, washed and dried. It still contain leaves, sticks and bug parts. Buttonlac has been filtered a bit. It has a rich, dark brown color. Garnet is a little lighter colored and has more red than buttonlac. Orange shellac is

Shellac With Wax

Dewaxed

probably the most familiar grade to consumers. Super blonde shellac is the most highly refined. It has most of the color and all the wax removed. All dry shellacs should be strained through a fine filter after mixing.

Seedlac

Buttonlac

Garnet

Orange

Super Blonde

Ready To Use

Zinsser's "Amber" shellac is a ready to use orange shellac and their "Clear" shellac is a blonde shellac. Both of these products contain wax and come as a 3-pound cut that should be thinned to a 1-2 pound cut before use.

"SealCoat" is a 2-pound cut of dewaxed blonde shellac. SealCoat is a universal sealer that adds just the right amount of warmth and color under a water-based finish.

Mixed shellac has a 6-month shelf life. Zinsser has found a way to stretch the shelf life of pre-mixed shellac to 3 years. Always look for the date of manufacture on the can before you buy. All three products are also available in handy spray cans.

Shellac's Many Advantages

- **Non-toxic** - Shellac is one of the safest finishes you can use. It is a naturally occurring material that's approved by the FDA to coat apples, candy and pharmaceuticals. When mixed with pure grain alcohol, shellac is free of toxic chemicals.
- **Repairable** - A damaged or worn shellac finish is easy to restore or repair.
- **Rubs out well** - Shellac is harder than most finishes. The hardness gives it excellent rubbing qualities.
- **Excellent moisture barrier** - If you want to keep wood movement to a minimum, shellac can't be beat.
- **Fast drying** - That means fewer troubles with dust settling into a wet film. You can usually recoat in under an hour for a fast build.
- **Universal sealant** - Dewaxed shellac can be used as a seal coat under almost any finish.
- **Less sanding** - Shellac does not require sanding between coats in order for one coat to adhere to another.

Smooth Out The Finish

Brushed-on shellac can "window pane," leaving fat thick edges. It can also "orange peel" when sprayed. This happens most often with heavy mix, so keeping your shellac thin (1-2lb. cut) is your best defense. If you are still having problems, try some "Shellac-Wet." Just a few drops in a quart of shellac will greatly improve flow-out and leveling. Do not use this additive if you plan to topcoat the shellac with a different finish, as it may cause adhesion problems.

Quick Mix Shellac

For quick repair work, or for those times when you didn't mix quite enough shellac there's "Gold Dust." It's basically pulverized shellac that's light yellow to amber in color. The powder is designed for fast, no-wait mixing of small batches.

The Right Mix

Using shellac that is mixed too thick is the #1 mistake people make. Until you gain experience using shellac, it's best to thin your shellac to a 1lb. cut (1-lb. of flakes dissolved in 1-gal. of alcohol). Old-time cabinetmakers used pure ethanol, or "spirits," to mix their shellac. Pure ethanol is still sold at liquor stores in some states as "Everclear" ($20 a quart). Make sure it's the 190-proof stuff. When mixed with dry shellac flakes Everclear produces an all-natural, non-toxic finish (safer than any water-based finish).

When the liquor store cashier wonders where the heck you're going with a case of 190-proof Everclear, just say, "I'm going to get shellacked"!

Denatured alcohol is the most common solvent for shellac. It costs a lot less than Everclear. It's essentially ethanol contaminated with another chemical to poison or "denature" the ethanol. This saves you from paying a liquor tax.

Specialty alcohols that contain no water (200

proof) are also available. These alcohols are blended to dissolve shellac a little quicker and dry a little slower, so it has more time to level out.

Control the Sheen

Most woodworkers are used to buying finishes with the desired sheen (gloss, semi-gloss, satin or flat) right off the shelf. With shellac you have one choice—high gloss. Traditionally shellac's sheen was adjusted by rubbing it out. Shellac is easy to rub to a glass smooth finish with the desired sheen. However, carved or heavily molded surfaces can be tricky to rub out. Thankfully, you can add a flattening agent like Shellac Flat to adjust the sheen. Shellac Flat is made with amorphous silica and alcohol.

Grind Your Own Flakes

Shellac flakes take quite a while to dissolve. When my shop is cool, I've had to wait more than 2-days. Too often I failed to plan ahead and have been forced to wait for my shellac to dissolve before work could progress.

You can greatly reduce the time it takes to mix shellac by grinding up the flakes. A simple blade-type coffee grinder does the trick. Warm temperatures also speed up the process. If your shop is on the cool side, find a warm place to mix your shellac. I've been known to put a jar in my car on a sunny day. In an hour or less the ground flakes are totally dissolved.

Shellac Flakes

Blade-Style Coffee Grinder

Mix Small Batches

I make shellac in small batches so it won't go bad before I can use it up. Mixed shellac's shelf life is about 6 months. After that it may not dry properly.

I use a small food scale (available at grocery stores) to weigh out the flakes. To mix one pint of 1-lb.-cut shellac, dissolve 2 oz. of shellac flakes in 16 oz. of alcohol. For a 2-lb. cut, double the flakes. After the shellac is fully dissolved, strain it through fine mesh cheesecloth or filter to remove impurities.

Use the Right Brush

Using the right brush is essential if you want your relationship with shellac to start off on the right foot. An inexpensive oval sash brush, like the Bestt Liebco #12 shown here, is perfect for applying shellac on trim work and molded edges. The natural china bristles easily wrap around contours without leaving big drips.

Golden Taklon is an amazing synthetic material used on brushes like the Athena 7100 Series. The bristles are wonderfully fine and soft and give you a precise edge and control.

A high-quality natural bristle brush with a chisel edge, like the Dunnet Fitch, is great for applying shellac on a large, flat surface like a tabletop.

Synthetic Golden Taklon

Oval Sash Brush

Natural Bristle Brush

Custom Colors

Shellac is easy to color. Whether you're looking for deep, soft brown or garish cadmium yellow, shellac can handle it. Just add alcohol-based dye. For pure colors, super-blonde shellac works best.

Finish Repair and Restoration

You're always better off to repair damage or any sound finish than you are to strip off the finish and start over. This section gives you detailed information on repairing finish damage, spot-removing the finish to repair the wood underneath, and practical methods for touching up the repair so no-one but you will ever spot it again. You'll also learn how to clean finishes, fill deep dings, and touch up scuffs.

When you must strip off the old finish, be sure to protect yourself from noxious chemicals: long sleeves, long neoprene gloves, solvent-proof apron, splash-proof goggles, and an activated-carbon respirator are recommended. More on page 134.

by KEVIN SOUTHWICK

Repair a Water-Damaged Finish

WORK MIRACLES ON WOOD WITH OXALIC ACID

Watering a potted plant can be disastrous if the plant lives on top of something made out of wood. We've all seen the white spots and black rings that can result when water seeps through the pot. And if you've ever tried to sand out these marks, you know it's a tough job that can leave tell-tale depressions on the surface. Fortunately, in many cases, this type of damage can be almost magically undone by treating the wood's surface with oxalic acid.

Oxalic acid removes the gray color from oxidized wood without changing the wood's natural color. That's why it's commonly used as the active ingredient in deck cleaners, and why restorers use it to remove gray or black water stains on furniture (see "Oxalic Acid Undoes Rust," next page). Oxalic acid is also used in some household cleaning products for removing hard water stains, and it has many industrial uses as well. Although it is found as a natural ingredient in some vegetables (spinach and rhubarb), oxalic acid is quite toxic if ingested in concentrated form.

The potted plant left a water stain that went right through the finish and into the wood.

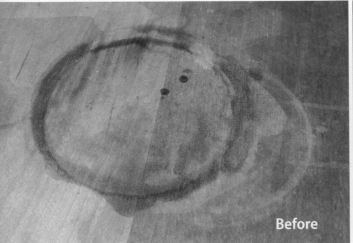

Before

After!

Identify the Stains

Every finish repair job is unique, of course, so the first step is to thoroughly examine the problem. The chest lid shown here has both whitish marks (also called blushing or bloom), and dark gray and black discolorations. White marks are usually in the finish; dark discolorations from water indicate more significant damage, because they're down in the wood.

To help formulate a plan to repair this finish, I dampened the entire lid with mineral spirits (paint thinner). This testing method is useful anytime you want to look closely at either old dry finish or bare wood. The look of the paint thinner-dampened surface is similar to how it would look if shellac or a clear oil based finish were applied. In this case, dampening the surface makes the whitish marks temporarily disappear (they reappear when the mineral spirits evaporates). That means a coat or two of finish is all that's needed to take care of the white marks. (This is a stroke of luck; if the white marks hadn't disappeared, additional repair steps would be necessary to remove them, and that's a topic for another story.)

Now I can focus on the black rings. The mineral spirits test shows that they get darker, and that makes them good candidates for treatment with oxalic acid. If the oxalic acid works, I won't have to aggressively sand the entire lid. Not only would sanding remove the remaining intact finish (80%, in this case), it would also lighten the lid's aged cherry color, so it would no longer match the rest of the chest that it belongs to.

Oxalic Acid Undoes Rust

Oxalic acid works a specific type of chemical magic by removing dark water stains from wood. These stains result when water containing iron and other minerals gets into wood. The discoloration that occurs is similar to rust. As shown here, oxalic acid is strong enough to dissolve the rust from an old plane iron, but it has little or no effect on the non-oxidized steel. (This plane iron soaked overnight in a saturated solution of oxalic acid.)

Oxalic acid is uniquely different from the other two bleaches occasionally used in wood finishing and refinishing, because neither chlorine bleach nor two-part bleach will significantly affect water stains or rust. Chlorine bleach is good for removing or lightening dyes (as it does in the laundry). Two-part bleach will lighten the color of just about anything it can soak into. Part A is sodium hydroxide (lye); Part B is hydrogen peroxide (which is also used to lighten hair color).

EDITOR: TIM JOHNSON

Start by thoroughly cleaning the surface. First, wipe it down with mineral spirits, to remove polish and other crud that's greasy or waxy. Mineral spirits also shows what the damaged areas will look like with a clear finish applied.

Dish Soap

When the mineral spirits has evaporated, complete the cleaning process by wiping the surface with soap and water, using a soft cloth, to remove water-soluble residue. Allow the surface to dry completely.

400-Grit Paper

Sand lightly, using fine paper, a soft block and very little pressure. Although the goal is to remove the raised grain from the damaged area, it's important to sand the entire surface to maintain consistency.

Plastic Spoon

Glass Jar

Saturated Solution

Mix a saturated solution of oxalic acid in a non-metal container. Add a spoonful at a time to the water and stir, until a layer of non-dissolved oxalic acid remains at the bottom.

Treat the Stains

Every step of this treatment should be done consistently to the entire surface, not just the damaged area. The procedure involves flooding the surface with water. Fortunately, the damage shown here is on solid wood—using this treatment on a veneered surface can be risky.

The first step is a thorough cleaning, using two different cleaners. Mineral spirits removes greasy residue, such as old wax or polish (Photo 1). Mild dish soap and water removes any water-soluble crud (Photo 2). Neither of these processes will damage an intact finish.

The grain is raised very slightly in the water-damaged area, so a little sanding with 400-grit paper is necessary (Photo 3). This step should take about one minute.

It's Already Gone!

Wipe on the oxalic acid solution. Leave it on the surface for about five minutes to achieve the maximum effect. Then wipe off the excess and let the surface dry thoroughly. The effect can be almost instantaneous.

Flood the surface with water repeatedly, to remove any remaining oxalic acid crystals.

Mix up a saturated solution of oxalic acid by adding the crystals to a jar of warm water with a plastic spoon (Photo 4). Do not use any metal containers or utensils—the acid could react with the metal. Add crystals a spoonful at a time and stir until no more will dissolve into the water. I always use a saturated solution, so that I have a maximum-strength problem solver.

Wearing gloves and eye protection, use a rag or sponge to saturate the entire surface being treated, not just the dark spots (Photo 5). Keep the surface wet for about five minutes to allow for the maximum effect. Then wipe off the excess and let the surface dry completely. You may see the effect immediately as you apply the acid, or the spots may disappear gradually, as the acid dries. If a second application of acid is necessary, wait to apply it until the first application has thoroughly dried, or

it won't work. If two or three applications do not remove the stain completely, more acid is not likely to help. You'll have to live with the remaining discoloration or resort to sanding to remove it. However, do not sand until you have thoroughly rinsed the surface—breathing dust that contains oxalic acid is extremely unpleasant and potentially hazardous.

When you've completed the oxalic applications, it's imperative to thoroughly rinse the treated surface with lots of clean water, to flush away any acid that remains on the wood (Photo 6). Flood the surface several times and dry it with a clean cloth or paper towel each time. Let the surface dry between each flooding.

Attempting to "neutralize" the acid that remains on the surface with a mild alkali such as baking soda, borax or ammonia is a cleansing option that is frequently mentioned as an alternative to rinsing. However, I have never seen any accurate formulas that would make this chemical balancing act a practical possibility. Besides, I know that thorough rinsing works.

After the lid has thoroughly dried, don a respirator and lightly sand the entire surface with 400-grit paper, to cut back any grain raised by the oxalic treatments. Test the surface again with mineral spirits, to gauge the results (Photo 7). The test on this lid indicates that the surface is ready for finishing (Photo 8).

Dampen the surface with mineral spirits to test the results. Here, the whitish blush areas virtually disappear and the black marks are 99.9% gone. The repair is complete; it's time to re-build the finish.

In this case, the finish is blonde shellac, the same finish as the original. Adding a waterproof finish over the shellac could help to prevent future damage. Moving the plant may be a better option.

FINISHING TIP

Test for Adhesion

How do you make sure that old can of finish will work with the new stuff you want to use as a topcoat? Lay one coat of finish over the other, in the order you plan to use them. Allow each coat to dry before proceeding. Then score the surface across the grain and see if you can lift one layer off the other with a sharp chisel. If you can, don't use them together.

James Dahlgren

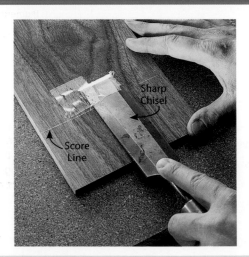

Sharp Chisel

Score Line

ART DIRECTION: JOEL SPIES • PHOTOGRAPHY: KRIVIT PHOTOGRAPHY
CONSULTANT: MICHAEL DRESDNER

by MICHAEL DRESDNER

Touch up: Repairing a Damaged Finish

HIDE BLEMISHES WITHOUT REFINISHING

Touch up refers to techniques used to repair and disguise damage on already finished wood—without refinishing. Whether you've rubbed through a finish, discovered glue spots or putty patches that stick out, or been faced with damage to the wood itself, knowing how to touch them up can save the day. Read on to discover the tools and techniques needed to masterfully disguise dings, dents and other blemishes.

Touch-up Tools

I'd like to tell you that you can just buy two or three felt-tip pens and a bunch of spray cans. Sadly, that's not the case. To accurately reproduce the wide range of colors that appear in finished wood, you'll have to mix them yourself, like an artist.

To do this you'll need to accumulate a variety of touch-up tools (Fig. A) and learn how to use them. You'll also need good lighting. Ideally, you should

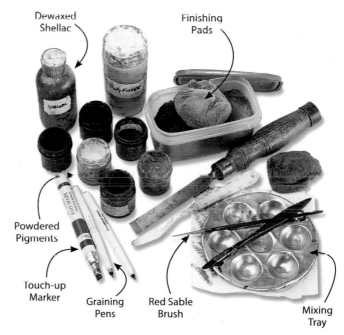

Dewaxed Shellac · Finishing Pads · Powdered Pigments · Touch-up Marker · Graining Pens · Red Sable Brush · Mixing Tray

Fig. A: Touch-Up Tools

This versatile touch-up kit includes the usual tools for patching dings as well as those for disguising the patch: shelf-stable powdered pigments; a mixing tray; fresh dewaxed shellac; one or more very fine, red sable brushes; graining pens; and furniture touch-up markers.

EDITOR • TIM JOHNSON; ART DIRECTION • JOEL SPIES; PHOTOGRAPHY • PHIL LEISENHEIMER

perform touch-up work in the same lighting (fluorescent, incandescent, direct, indirect, etc.) under which the piece will be viewed. The next best choice is daylight, or artificial, full-spectrum light.

Repair the Damage

If you are touching up a light sand-through or glue spot where both background color and grain are still intact, you can skip to the section called "Adjust the Color," on page 126.

Auto body filler is well suited for use in wood repairs. It is a catalyzed, high-strength adhesive that cures fast, smooths well and takes a finish. Drop it into the center of the damaged area with a palette knife and work it out to the edges to ensure a good bond (Photo 2). Add more to the center until the patch is over-filled. When the filler has started to harden, but before it has completely cured, shave it flat to the surface with a sharp chisel (Photo 3). If you notice any voids, simply add more filler and shave it down. After the filler has cured, sand it smooth with fine sandpaper, and you're ready to begin the touch-up process.

Wood putty can also be used for repairs, just be sure it is one or two shades lighter than the lightest color you can see in the wood. It's quite difficult to hide a darker patch—it always shows up as a shadow.

Seal First, Then Color

As a first step, and again in between each layer of color, seal the touch-up area with a bit of clear finish. This shows you the true color of the surface under a finish so

Oh, no! When a finish gets dinged, don't panic. Damage like this can be touched up.

Fill the hole. Use a palette knife to drop auto body or wood filler into the center of the damaged area, then work it firmly to the edges.

you can match the touch up correctly. It also provides a base for each layer of color. I like to use thin, dewaxed shellac for the sealer, applied with a small brush, a cotton cloth formed into a pad, or a spray can. Let the sealer dry at least 10 minutes before you continue.

After sealing, check the background color. If it's correct, go directly to the graining step. If the patch is too light, mix a color one shade lighter than the lightest

Pare the patch flush. A sharp chisel pares the semi-hardened body filler flush with the surface.

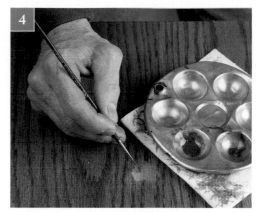

Add background color. Brush a thin, but opaque mix of powdered pigments and shellac to color the patch.

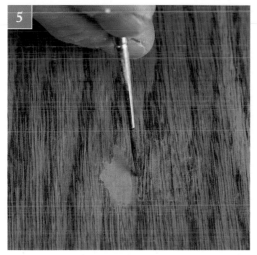

Add grain lines. Connect the wood's grain across the patch with a good, sharp-pointed brush.

background color in the area around the patch. Use a brush to create a small puddle of shellac on the mixing tray. Dip the brush into whichever pigments you need and add them to the shellac until you have a thin but opaque "paint," thinning it with alcohol as needed. If it is too thick it will build up a "scab" of color. Apply the pigment and shellac mixture with a small brush, taking care not to make the touch up larger than it needs to be (Photo 4).

Add the Grain Lines

As before, seal the color coat and let the shellac dry. Simply put, adding grain lines is painting a picture of the wood onto the patch. Using your finest brush, mix a dark color to match the grain of the wood and copy the missing grain pattern (Photo 5). A good, red sable brush that comes to a fine, sharp point allows you to control the color in thin lines. Use short, careful strokes. If you are not comfortable with a brush, most suppliers also sell fine-point felt-tip markers specifically for graining.

Work on the graining until you are satisfied with it. If it starts to get away from you, erase it with some 0000 steel wool and start over. You can do this because you sealed the previous color coat. When you are satisfied with them, seal over the grain lines before continuing. Note: Even though you have not changed the background color, adding the grain lines makes the overall patch appear darker. That's why you start with a background a shade lighter.

Voilà! Fine-tune the color match, build the finish and rub out the sheen to match the surrounding area.

Adjust the Color

Take a careful look at the spot, stepping back and viewing it from several angles. If the grain lines look right, but the patch is still too light overall, add a thin translucent layer of color to blend the spot. When you're touching up a glue spot or an area sanded through that still retains the grain lines and background color, this will be the only step you need to take.

Mix a small amount of pigment into a puddle of shellac—just enough to tint it but not enough to make it opaque. Imagine that this "wash" is a translucent, colored film that you will lay on top of the patch. This wash should be a weak but fairly dark tint, since you are blending the color already there. For that reason, you should be able to add thin coats over the grain lines as well without making them lighter or muddier. You can

also use touch-up markers, or even a mixture of alcohol-soluble dye and shellac instead of pigment. Take it slow on this step. It is easy to go too dark and undo all your fine artistic work.

When the touch-up is virtually invisible, seal it again with several coats of shellac. Let the touched-up area dry overnight if you plan to add another type of finish. Make sure you have enough shellac over the last color coat to allow you to rub out the area to match the sheen of the rest of the piece (Photo 6).

One final comment: The object of touch-up is to fool the eye by camouflaging the repaired area. The truth is you will always be able to spot your own touch-up, no matter how good it is, but those who don't know it's there will never see it.

Iron Out Those Dents

Here's a classic tip that *everyone* should know: It's not hard to make a dent in wood and fortunately, it's not hard to get one out, either. All you need is a household iron (don't worry, it won't get wrecked, but you may want to ask permission if it's not yours) and a damp cloth. Put a couple drops of water onto the dent and let it soak for a minute. Then lay the damp cloth over the dent and press the hot iron over it. The water in and around the dent is heated to steam which quickly swells the wood fibers back to their original shape. Don't over do it with the iron. Once you see the steam, remove the iron and cloth and give the fibers a little time to swell. If the dent isn't completely gone after the first try, repeat the process. A little light sanding completes the repair.

Dave Munkittrick

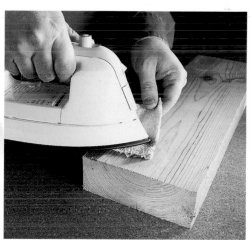

A household iron and a damp rag are all you need to repair most dings and dents.

Dang!

All Better

Yes, these really are genuine before and after photos.

ART DIRECTION: JOEL SPIES • PHOTOGRAPHY: KRIVIT PHOTOGRAPHY • CONSULTANT: MICHAEL DRESDNER

by BOB FLEXNER

Tips for Repairing Finishes

RESCUE BATTLE-SCARRED FINISHES WITH ORDINARY MATERIALS

Remove Stickers and Tape

Stickers and tape may not neatly peel off if they've been stuck to a finish for a long time. Here are several methods for removing them.

If a sticker is made from paper, wet it for a few minutes and try rubbing it off with your finger. If this doesn't work, or if you're dealing with tape, try heating with a blow drier or heat gun to soften the adhesive. (Be very careful with a heat gun because it can blister the finish.) Once the bulk of the sticker or tape is gone, remove the remaining adhesive with naphtha, toluene or xylene. (Don't use acetone or lacquer thinner; they may damage the finish.) Products designed to remove latex paint spatter, such as Oops! and Goof Off, may also work. None of these solvents will damage any finish except a water-based one, but try them out on a hidden area first. If the sticker or tape is very stubborn, try working one of these solvents under it.

If these methods don't work, you'll have to sand or scrape off the sticker or tape and repair the finish.

Rub Out White Marks

White marks may be caused by water or heat. Water-created marks are easier to repair because the damage usually doesn't go very deep.

Water marks are usually caused by sweaty glasses. They're almost always confined to the finish's surface, so they're easy to remove by rubbing with an abrasive. If the surface is glossy, try rottenstone and mineral oil on a cloth, or toothpaste on your finger. If these abrasives don't cut fast enough, use 0000 steel wool to cut through the damage quickly, then restore the finish's gloss by rubbing with rottenstone and mineral oil. If the surface is satin or flat, abrade with 0000

steel wool and mineral oil. If you can't get the sheen of the damaged area to match the rest of the surface, rub the entire surface with the same abrasive.

White marks caused by heat damage go deeper into the finish than those created by water. They're more difficult, and sometimes impossible, to remove by abrasion. You may have to strip and refinish.

Remove Dirty Discoloration

Discoloration around drawer and cabinet-door pulls, or on chair arms and backs, may simply be dirt that's easy to wash off with soap and water. On the other hand, it may be dirt mixed with deteriorated finish. In that case, the finish may have to be removed and replaced.

The first thing to do is to wash the dirty area with a mild soap and warm water. Ordinary liquid dishwashing soaps are best. If this doesn't remove the discoloration, the finish is probably deteriorated. Many finishes break down under extended contact with acidic body oils. In addition to being discolored, the finish may be soft enough to scrape away with your fingernail.

Sometimes you can remove the top layers of a deteriorated finish using fine sandpaper or steel wool, but if the finish has deteriorated to the wood, you usually have to strip and refinish the entire surface.

Match Colors On Glass

Replacing missing color usually involves color matching, which most people find difficult. To make it easier, do the color matching on a small piece of glass or rigid, clear plastic placed on a part of the surface you're matching. Use an artist's brush to mix several colors

until the blend matches the color underneath the glass or plastic. Brush the colorant onto the damage and protect it by applying a finish.

For the colorant, you can use concentrated oil, acrylic, universal or Japan colors, available from woodworking suppliers and paint and hobby stores. Or you can blend ready-made stains.

Touch Up a Scuffed Edge

Sharp edges are easily scraped. A scrape may not damage the wood, but it often removes the wood's stained color, leaving a light area that stands out like a sore thumb. To repair the damage, simply drag an appropriately colored felt-tip marker over the damage. If the marker is pointed, use its side. This fix also works well with new finishes if you've accidentally sanded through a stained edge.

Felt-tip markers in various wood tones are available from most woodworking suppliers and home centers. "Magic" markers rarely match wood tones so they are seldom a good choice.

After the marker repair is thoroughly dry, apply some finish to protect the color from being rubbed off. Wiping varnish is easy to apply and won't smear the color. You can make your own by thinning any regular or polyurethane varnish with mineral spirits. Mix equal parts of varnish and thinner. Dampen a cloth wrapped around your finger with this mixture and drag it along the repaired edge.

Remove Crazing and Light Scratches

Film finishes craze with age. That is, they develop a tight pattern of cracks similar to what you'd see on an old oil painting. If the cracks are shallow, and don't penetrate through a layer of color, they may be sanded out. Light scratches can be removed in the same way.

Choose a sandpaper grit coarse enough to efficiently cut through the damage but not so coarse that you create large scratches or risk sanding through to the wood. The best choices are usually 320- or 400-grit stearated sandpaper (3M Tri-M-ite or Norton 3X), or 600- or 1000-grit wet/dry (black) sandpaper. Use stearated sandpaper dry and wet/dry sandpaper with a lubricant of mineral oil or mineral spirits. Dry sanding lets you see your progress better so you are less likely to sand through.

Begin by sanding a small part of the surface to test that you're using the correct grit. Then sand the entire surface. Back the sandpaper with a flat block only if the surface is flat, or you may sand through high spots. When you have removed the crazing or scratches, rub out the finish or apply new finish (see "Revive A Dull Finish," next page).

Remove Felt-Tip Pen Marks

Felt-tip pen ink almost always dissolves in alcohol, acetone or lacquer thinner. Any of these solvents can be used to remove marks

on a wood finish, but because acetone and lacquer thinner damage most finishes, it's best to use denatured alcohol. Shellac is the only finish this solvent will damage.

To remove an ink mark, simply dampen a cloth with denatured alcohol and wipe it lightly over the colored area. To reduce any chance of damage, avoid making the finish wet with alcohol. A light wipe or two should remove all of the ink.

Revive A Dull Finish

All finishes dull as they age, but you can usually bring back their shine. The easiest way is to apply paste wax. If the dulling has progressed too far, however, you must rub the finish with fine abrasives or apply another coat or two of finish.

To rub a finish, choose an abrasive that produces the sheen you want. You can use a powder, such as rottenstone or pumice, steel wool or a commercial rubbing compound. Rottenstone produces a glossy finish; pumice and 0000 steel wool produce a satin finish. Use mineral oil or mineral spirits as a lubricant with rottenstone, pumice or steel wool. Commercial rubbing compounds don't require an additional lubricant.

If you must recoat the finish, be sure the surface is clean. Wash it with mineral spirits to remove grease and wax. Wash it with soap and water to remove sticky dirt. Then apply the finish you originally used, or apply oil, shellac, water-based finish, or any type of varnish, including polyurethane. Lacquer is risky to apply because lacquer thinner may cause the old finish to blister.

Repair Color Damage

There are at least four methods of repairing color damage in finished wood. The first step is to determine which method works best. To do this, apply a liquid to the damage and see what happens.

The best liquid to use is mineral spirits. It won't damage any finish, and it penetrates any wax that might be on the surface to give a more accurate diagnosis. Liquid from your mouth also works well, so I call this the "spit test." When you dab any of these liquids, one of four things will happen:

1. The color comes back. That's great, because the solution is merely to apply some finish.
2. The color only partially comes back. You'll have to stain before putting on more finish.
3. The color doesn't change. Stain won't work. You'll have to "paint" in the color with a colored marker or artist's brush before applying finish.
4. The color gets too dark. The best fix is to apply clear paste wax, or seal the damage with a fast-drying finish such as shellac, then coat with the finish of your choice.

Fill Gouges With Epoxy

The easiest method of filling dents and gouges is using an epoxy stick. Sticks are available in a variety of colors from most woodworking suppliers and home centers. Here's how to do it.

First, level the surface. That is, remove all roughness at the top edge of the gouge. Then cut enough material from the epoxy stick to do the job. You can blend different colors to match your wood. Knead the epoxy until it's a uniform color.

Press the epoxy into the gouge leaving a slight rise above the wood's surface. Dampen the epoxy with water, then remove the excess by scraping the filled area with a credit card or plastic putty knife. You can also level the epoxy by sanding after it hardens, backing your sandpaper with a small flat block. Sanding usually damages the finish around the fill, though.

by MICHAEL DRESDNER

Successful Stripping

YOU CAN DO IT SAFELY AND EFFECTIVELY. HERE'S HOW.

L et's face it; stripping wood is a drag. We approach it knowing it's a difficult, messy job, but hoping we can reclaim a jewel from the muck. Knowing what to use and how to use it is essential to success. Here's a run through of the three basic types of strippers and how to use them safely and effectively.

Suit up as if for chemical warfare, and work outdoors or in a well-ventilated place.

Safety First

It's impossible to talk about stripping without talking about safety. Some strippers require less protection than others, but always err on the side of safety and follow these guidelines:

- Protect your body with long sleeves and a solvent-proof apron.
- Wear splash-proof goggles; not just safety glasses.
- Use long, neoprene gloves and turn back the ends into cuffs, so that when you lift your arms, the stripper drips into the cuff, not onto your arm.
- Work only in areas with good ventilation or outdoors. You should never be able to smell the fumes.
- Wear an activated-carbon respirator with working cartridges.

Some strippers, especially those called "refinishers," are highly flammable. If the can says the stripper is flammable, keep sparks and flames away from your work area. If you use a fan that is not explosion proof (it has an exposed motor, for example), position it so that you are between the fan and the window or door.

The Basic Equipment For Safe Stripping Includes:

- A fan for ventilation
- Long neoprene gloves, with cuffs rolled back to keep goop from running down your arm
- Solvent-proof apron, either heavy cloth, plastic, or rubber
- Organic-cartridge respirator (with some strippers)
- Splash-proof goggles (if they're not part of the respirator)
- Tools for removing the gunk: a dull putty knife, scrub pads and brushes, wood shavings, string, wooden sticks, and scrapers
- A big, sloppy, old brush and a can or bowl for applying and holding the stripper
- Solvents for washing the stripped surface; water or alcohol, lacquer thinner and mineral spirits, depending on the stripper
- Plastic bags or sheeting to cover your piece while the stripper works.

Have the fan push clean air toward you, and the vapors away from both you and the fan. That way you will not be drawing vapor-filled air through a spark-producing fan motor.

Finally, if you have heart disease, avoid using strippers that contain methylene chloride. Inhaling methylene chloride reduces the amount of oxygen in the blood, and can trigger an attack in people with heart disease. Even for healthy people, methylene chloride-based strippers require powerful ventilation.

Choose a Stripper

Except for "refinishers," which are only for shellac and lacquer, most strippers will remove just about any finish. Choose a stripper based on its speed and safety. A good rule of thumb is: The safer it is, the slower it works. As shown in "Choosing a Stripper," page 139, you can choose fast and hazardous, moderately fast and moderately hazardous, or slow and safe. Be aware that the safety requirements for each stripper may be different; read labels carefully.

There are modern finishes that won't budge for any stripper, but they're rare. Some very old pieces may have a thin milk-based paint on them that is also resistant to normal strippers. However, it will come off with a strong lye wash.

Set Up Your Work Area

After choosing your stripper, gather together your stripping paraphernalia (see "The Basic Equipment," page 135). Dismantle the piece as far as is practical, and remove any hardware, making certain you label all the parts carefully for reassembly. I sometimes do a numbered sketch for complicated pieces, and number parts in hidden areas, such as inside the joints. You might even want to take "before" photos.

Put on the Stripper

The key to easy stripping is to apply a lot of stripper, convince it to stay on, and give it plenty of time to work, without interruption. Many strippers contain a wax that will rise to the surface and form a crust to prevent the active solvent from evaporating. If you brush the stripper, you disturb the crust and allow the solvent to evaporate.

Shake the can of stripper gently before use, then cover the cap with a rag or paper towel. Unscrew it slowly because sometimes the stripper spurts out. Apply the stripper thickly (Photo 2) and try to keep the work horizontal so the stripper doesn't run.

I've found the most effective way to keep the stripper wet and active is to seal the workpiece in plastic. You can use a leaf bag (Photo 3), or a tent of polyethylene film

Strippers made of solvent mixtures work from the top down (left), melting the finish into a soft goo. Methylene chloride strippers work by dropping through the finish (right) to break the bond between it and the wood.

Apply the stripper in a thick layer, ⅛- to ¼-in. thick. On vertical surfaces, semi-paste removers work best because they cling. Once on, leave the stripper alone and let it do the work.

available in rolls from your home center. Use duct tape to seal the plastic, keeping the tape on the outside. Do a dry-run first, to make sure the plastic covers the piece completely.

For fast methylene chloride strippers, an hour in the bag should do the trick. Allow two to three hours for the moderately fast strippers, and overnight for 3M's Safest Stripper. If you aren't sure, put the stripper on late in the day, bag your work, and leave it overnight.

Seal your work in a bag. If the piece is too big for a bag, cover it with a tent made of polyethylene sheeting. I like to put several layers of newspapers under the work to catch the drips.

Scoop off the finish using a putty knife with a dull edge and rounded corners.

The bag method works for all except caustic strippers, which should be checked periodically and the gunk removed as soon as the wood comes clean, to prevent possible damage to the wood. The other strippers can remain on the wood for long periods without damaging it.

Take it All Off

Before you remove the bag, open the windows, turn on the fan, put on your goggles, gloves, apron and respirator. Open the bag carefully. The finish should virtually fall off right down to the bare wood. Scoop it off (Photos 4 and 5), using whatever tool works without damaging the wood. If you're using a water-based stripper, don't use metal tools or steel wool; they can leave rust marks on the wood.

As you remove the sludge, spread it out on newspaper. The object is to let it dry out before you dispose of it. If the stripper on your piece starts to dry before you get it off, add more stripper with your brush or pad. If the finish still doesn't come completely off, recoat the wood, tie up the bag, and repeat the process.

Washing the Wood

Before the wood has a chance to dry, wash off any last bits of paint or residue from the stripper. For methylene chloride strippers, use a mix of equal parts of denatured alcohol, mineral spirits, and lacquer thinner applied with a nylon pad. For other strippers, use the solvent recommended on the container.

Finally, repeat the scrub with a solution of one cup household ammonia in a quart of warm water. This will remove silicone or other oils that can interfere with both solvent- and water-based finishes.

Note: If you're using a refinisher, neither of these washes is necessary. Apply your new finish directly to the stripped wood.

Cleaning Up

Clean scrubbers, brushes, gloves, and other tools in the remaining solvent wash. Put your messy plastic, newspapers with finish gunk, and solvent-soaked rags outside in the fresh air to dry, away from people and pets. Let used solvent wash evaporate. This will go quickly if you pour it onto a pile of wood shavings spread on newspaper or plastic, someplace where there is no risk of fire.

Dry residue from household stripping projects, unless it includes lead paint, is usually considered safe to throw out with the trash. Any residue containing lead paint, and all liquid residue should be treated as hazardous waste. Contact your local health, environmental, or sanitation authorities for disposal instructions.

Wood shavings help scrub sludge from turnings and carvings. Other useful tools include string for getting into cracks and turnings, plastic scrub brushes, and pointed dowels for tight corners. The bag and newspaper act as a drop cloth and clean-up aid.

The wood is washed clean with the recommended solvent to remove any bits of paint and any remaining stripper. I recommend a final wash of one cup ammonia in a quart of water, then an overnight drying.

Choosing a Stripper

Fast But Hazardous Strippers

Refinishers work only on plain lacquer or shellac. They dissolve the finish instantly, but are highly flammable. They're used differently than other strippers: Wearing gloves, goggles and respirator, soak steel wool or an abrasive pad with refinisher, scrub the surface, and wipe off the finish as it liquifies. The finish will start melting almost immediately. Repeat until you are down to bare wood.

Methylene chloride (also called dichloromethane or DCM) strippers soften a finish in as little as 10 minutes. They work from the bottom up, so the finish comes off in sheets (Photo 1). Because they work by making the finish let go of the wood, you often need to use less of this stripper than other types. This type of stripper is non-flammable, but its vapor is harmful. Wear an activated-carbon respirator and have plenty of ventilation.

Medium-Fast and Moderately Hazardous Strippers

Solvent mixtures may contain small amounts of methylene chloride mixed with other solvents, or new non-flammable stripping agents like n-methyl-2-pyrrolidone and gamma butyrolactone. You still must wear gloves and goggles, and most require ventilation. These strippers work from the top down (see Photo 1). For many folks they represent a happy medium, being relatively safe yet relatively fast.

Caustic strippers are strong alkalines like lye. Although water-based and non-flammable, they can seriously burn your skin and eyes, so wear goggles and gloves, and be careful not to splash. Because caustic strippers are water-based, they raise the wood grain and can loosen joints and veneer. They also may darken the wood, so they're often used when the wood will be repainted. Unlike other strippers, you can't leave them on longer than necessary, or the wood itself may get damaged.

Slow and Safe

Safest Stripper, made by 3M, is the only very safe stripper. It can be used indoors with no special ventilation and no gloves (although if your skin is sensitive, you may want to wear them anyway). Safest Stripper is particularly effective on oil-based paint and polyurethane. However, it can take as long as 24 hours to soften a finish. Safest Stripper seems to pull oil-based finish out of the pores better than other strippers, so it's handy for woods like oak and ash. Because it's water-based, it will raise the wood grain and can loosen veneer.

FINISHING TIP

Seal Porous End Grain with Epoxy

Outdoor furniture will last longer if the legs can't wick up moisture from the ground. A thin-bodied epoxy soaks in the best. Hobby stores usually carry it in several formulations. Just pick the runniest one. It'll probably have an extended open time. If you get too exuberant and drip epoxy over the edges, clean it off with acetone before it cures.

Tim Johnson

Chair Leg

ART DIRECTION: SHELLEY MOEN • PHOTOGRAPHY: MIKE HABERMANN

FINISHING TIP

Make Your Own Wood Putty

Tired of never having fresh wood putty when you need it? You've probably opened a can and found its contents dried out, unusable or the wrong color.

If you plan to use a clear finish, you can make your own putty from sanding dust (save some when you're sanding your project) and varnish. Just mix the two into a thick dough by adding the varnish to the dust, a little at a time. Varnish makes a good binder. Even though it takes a long time, once dry, it stays dry. Shellac and lacquer may dry faster, but putty made with them tends to dissolve under a fresh topcoat of the same finish.

Apply the dough with a putty knife and let it dry (at least overnight) before sanding. Under a clear finish, this putty closely matches the wood tone, although it may be a slightly darker color.

Tim Johnson

Homemade Putty

Sanding Dust

Varnish

ART DIRECTION: SHELLEY MOEN • PHOTOGRAPHY: MIKE HABERMANN

FINISHING TIP

Make Surface Checks Disappear

Don't let small surface checks keep you from using an otherwise good board. Got a minute? You can make those checks disappear.

Squeeze cyanoacrylate (CA) glue into the crack. CA glue works better than yellow glue because it dries very quickly. Any brand of gap-filling CA glue with a 5- to 15-second open time will work (about $5 at home centers and hardware stores). Use a tip with a pin-sized hole (you can get replacement tips for 50 cents at hobby stores).

Immediately sand the area, mixing sanding dust with the glue and packing it in the cavity. Keep sanding until the crack is filled and the excess glue is removed. You may need to repeat the process. Under a finish, the sanding dust/glue mixture is almost invisible.

Tim Johnson

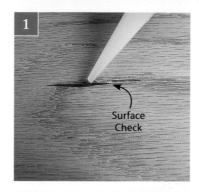

Surface Check

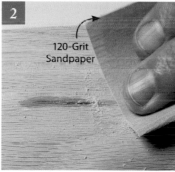

120-Grit Sandpaper

ART DIRECTION: SHELLEY MOEN • PHOTOGRAPHY: MIKE HABERMANN

FINISHING TIP

Bag Your Cartridge Mask

Organic vapor cartridges work great but they're useful life is only about eight hours. That's not very long. And what's worse, they're such dedicated little buggers they actually keep right on working even when you're not wearing the mask. Give them a rest and prolong their life by storing your mask in an airtight container when not in use. A resealable plastic bag or an old ice-cream pail work great.

Dave Munkittrick

ART DIRECTION: JOEL SPIES • PHOTOGRAPHY: KRIVIT PHOTOGRAPHY
CONSULTANT: MICHAEL DRESDNER

Index

More Great Books from Fox Chapel Publishing

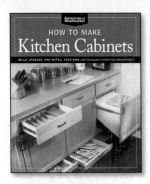

**How To Make
Kitchen Cabinets**
ISBN 978-1-56523-506-9 **$24.95**

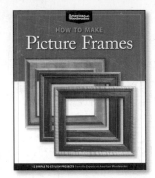

How to Make Picture Frames
ISBN 978-1-56523-459-8 **$19.95**

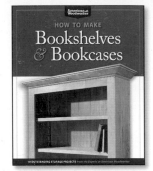

**How to Make
Bookshelves & Bookcases**
ISBN 978-1-56523-458-1 **$19.95**

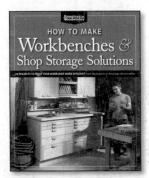

**How to Make Workbenches
& Shop Storage Solutions**
ISBN 978-1-56523-595-3 **$24.95**

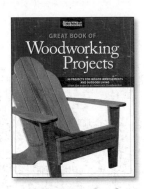

**Great Book of
Woodworking Projects**
ISBN 978-1-56523-504-5 **$24.95**

**Illustrated Guide
to Furniture Repair
& Refinishing**
ISBN 978-1-56523-527-4 **$24.99**

Look for These Books at Your Local Bookstore or Specialty Retailer or at www.FoxChapelPublishing.com